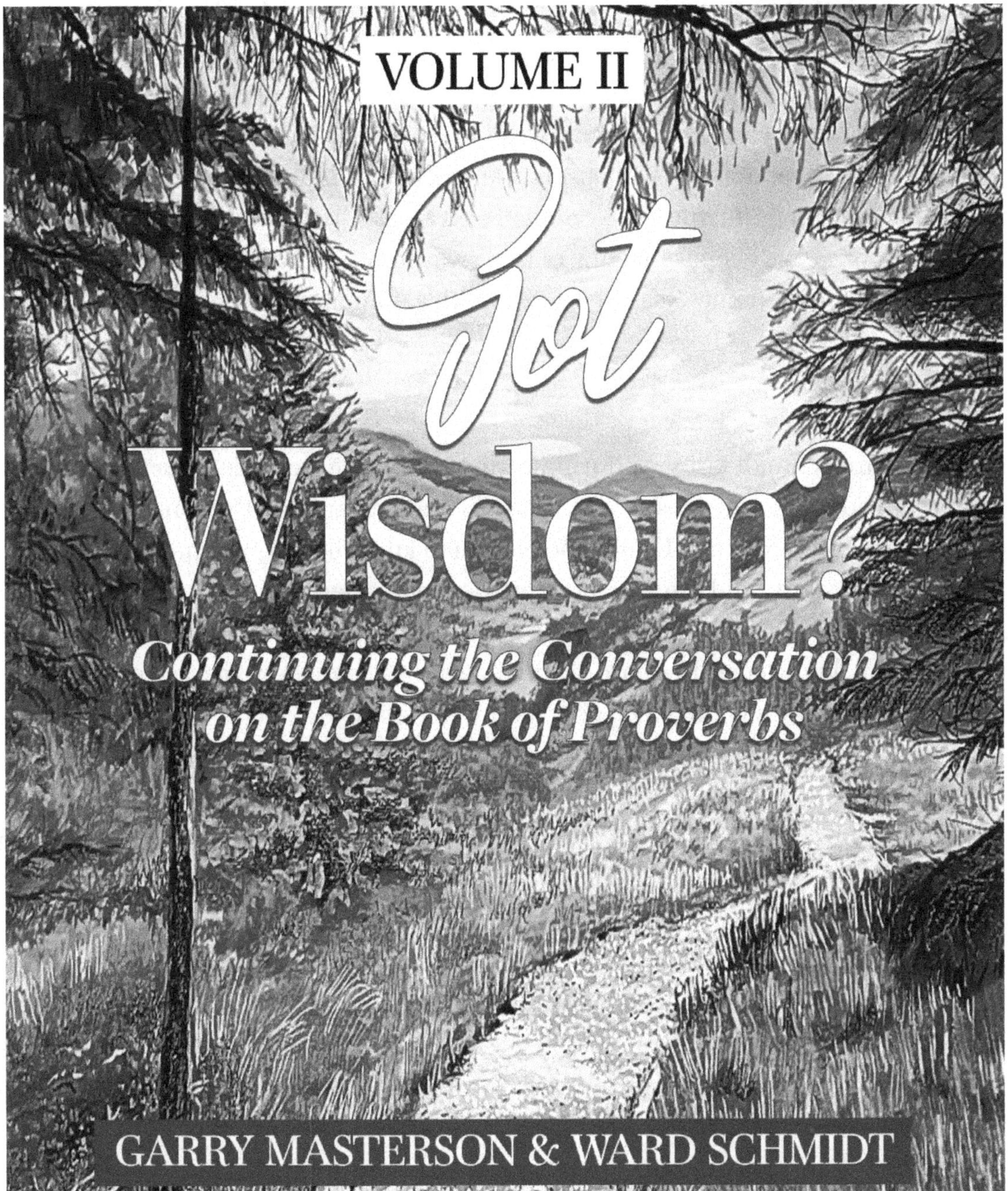

VOLUME II
Got Wisdom?
Continuing the Conversation on the Book of Proverbs

GARRY MASTERSON & WARD SCHMIDT

PRAISE FOR GOT WISDOM? VOLUME II

How often have you heard the admonishment to read the Bible daily? To meditate on the words and their meaning. *Got Wisdom?* is a kind invitation to do just that! Proverbs is a guide to help each of us pursue the wisdom of God and His righteousness. Ward and Garry invite us to look at the deeper meeting of God's wisdom. You will enjoy taking that extra step towards understanding. Really goes well with caffeinated coffee!

—*Bill Scheel*
Friend of the Author

I first met Ward Schmidt last year during a trip to Cuba, where his love for God and other people was evident in how he shared the gospel and encouraged the congregation of the local church we were visiting. I have since gotten to know him better through our church and men's bible study, and I'm always impressed by his deep knowledge of the Bible. No matter what we're discussing, he seems to have the relevant bible references in his head and additional knowledge to share from his studies and life experience. I'm always interested in what he's got to say, and I can't think of anyone better suited to add their commentary to the Book of Proverbs.

—*Micah Siesennop*
Board Chair, Neighbors in Action, Inc.

One of the joys of ministry is sharing it with others. I have been privileged to work with Ward Schmidt for many years and have witnessed his deep faith and compassion for others. He loves God's Word, studies it profusely, and then goes out and shares it with the people he meets. Whether living on the streets, in a classroom setting, or merely an acquaintance from another country, Ward always has a well-thought-out, kind word of faith for everyone.

—*Ann Spears*
Former Associate Pastor, First Methodist Church, Houston, TX

Garry Masterson has worked diligently to create for many people—both Christians and those who are curious—a conversation where they can take the writings of the book of Proverbs and learn the meanings often hidden in the verses. Far too many people just read the Bible and never really take the time to dig into the history of the time or the meanings that are sometimes lost when translating from the original Hebrew text into English. You also get to read the interpretations from some devoted Christians who have dedicated their lives to the Lord, just like Garry and Cindy have done. Thank you for allowing me to contribute in some small way.

—*Rev. John Burchell*

This detailed look at Proverbs by Garry Masterson gives an insightful commentary on how each verse is relevant to Christians today. He brings readers to contemplate the richness of each verse and prods us to make a step closer to God. He includes comments, thoughts, and reactions from a group of believers, allowing the reader to engage with the group, see other perspectives, and realize how the Lord connects with us. Fellow sojourners will be inspired!

—*Cindi Cicio*

The book of Proverbs is a very relevant topic that is hardly ever preached. I just received the first volume and can't stop reading it. Ward adds extra insight into the text, sometimes bringing to the surface memories from his childhood, experiences from his warm home, and practical ideas, which makes it very personal and enjoyable to read. I have been a Bible teacher for years, leading and guiding groups through most of the Mediterranean countries. I understand the importance of finding and creating a connection between the text and the reader. Ward really accomplished this well. This book offers a fresh perspective on an Old Testament classic and makes a great gift for any occasion.

—*Hannaniah Pinto*
Co-founder of Biblical Resources, La Grange, GA,
Author of *Jesus' Last Night with His Disciples*

Proverbs is my favorite book in the Bible. *Got Wisdom? Volume II* is written in an excellent format to help people from all walks of life apply the wisdom to their own lives, no matter what they're going through. I feel like the way that the authors included input from people with different backgrounds is clever, as well. Diverse points of view make for an enriching experience. This book is perfect for both individual and group study.

—Doreen Van Dyke
Natural Wellness Advisor and Outdoor Enthusiast

Copyright © 2025 by Garry Masterson and Ward Schmidt

All rights reserved. No portion of this publication may be reproduced, stored in an electronic system, or transmitted in any form by any means, electronic, mechanical, photocopy, recording, or otherwise, without the author's prior permission, except with brief quotations used in literary reviews and specific non-commercial uses permitted by copyright law. For permission requests, please use the contact information at the back of this book.

The views expressed in this book are the author's and do not necessarily reflect those of the publisher.

Unless otherwise indicated, the Scripture references in this book are taken from The Holy Bible, English Standard Version®. ESV® Text Edition: 2016. Copyright © 2001 by Crossway Bibles, a publishing ministry of Good News Publishers. All rights reserved.

Scripture references marked as "AMP" are taken from the Amplified Bible Copyright © 2015 by The Lockman Foundation, La Habra, CA 90631. All rights reserved.

Scripture references marked as "CEB" are taken from the Common English Bible (CEB) Copyright © 2011 by Common English Bible. All rights reserved.

Scripture references marked as "CEV" are taken from the Contemporary English Version® Copyright © 1995 by American Bible Society. All rights reserved.

Scripture references marked as "CJB" are taken from the Complete Jewish Bible, Copyright © 1998 by David H. Stern. All rights reserved.

Scripture references marked as "CPDV" are taken from the Catholic Public Domain Version Bible (public domain).

Scripture references marked as "EASY" are taken from the EasyEnglish Bible Copyright © MissionAssist 2019–Charitable Incorporated Organisation 1162807. Used by permission. All rights reserved.

Scripture references marked as "FBV" are taken from the Free Bible Version, which is a project of Free Bible Ministry, licensed through creativecommons.org and used with the author's permission. www.freebibleministry.org

Scripture references marked as "GNT" are taken from the Good News Translation. Good News Translation® (Today's English Version, Second Edition) Copyright © 1992 American Bible Society. All rights reserved.

Scripture references marked as "GW" are taken from the GOD'S WORD Translation. Copyright © 1995, 2003, 2013, 2014, 2019, 2020 by God's Word to the Nations Mission Society. All rights reserved.

Scripture references marked as "ICB" are taken from The Holy Bible, International Children's Bible® Copyright© 1986, 1988, 1999, 2015 by Thomas Nelson. Used by permission.

Scripture references marked as "KJV" are taken from the King James Version (public domain).

Scripture references marked as "MEV" are taken from The Holy Bible, Modern English Version. Copyright © 2014 by Military Bible Association. Published and distributed by Charisma House. All rights reserved.

Scripture references marked as "MSG" are taken from *THE MESSAGE*, Copyright © 1993, 2002, 2018 by Eugene H. Peterson. Used by permission of NavPress. All rights reserved. Represented by Tyndale House Publishers, Inc.

Scripture references marked as "NCV" are taken from The Holy Bible, New Century Version®. Copyright © 2005 by Thomas Nelson, Inc.

Scripture references marked as "NET" are taken from the New England Translation, NET Bible® Copyright © 1996-2017 by Biblical Studies Press, L.L.C. http://netbible.com All rights reserved.

Scripture references marked as "NIRV" are taken from the New International Reader's Version, Copyright © 1995, 1996, 1998, 2014 by Biblica, Inc.®. Used by permission. All rights reserved worldwide.

Scripture references marked as "NIV" are taken from the Holy Bible, New International Version®, NIV® Copyright ©1973, 1978, 1984, 2011 by Biblica, Inc.® Used by permission. All rights reserved worldwide.

Scripture references marked as "NKJV" are taken from the New King James Version®. Copyright © 1982 by Thomas Nelson. Used by permission. All rights reserved.

Scripture references marked as "NLT" are taken from the *Holy Bible*, New Living Translation, copyright © 1996, 2004, 2015 by Tyndale House Foundation. Used by permission of Tyndale House Publishers, Inc., Carol Stream, Illinois 60188. All rights reserved.

Scripture references marked as "NLV" are taken from the *Holy Bible*, New Living Translation, Copyright © 1996, 2004, 2015 by Tyndale House Foundation. Used by permission of Tyndale House Publishers, Inc., Carol Stream, Illinois 60188. All rights reserved.

Scripture references marked as "RSV" are taken from the Revised Standard Version of the Bible, Copyright © 1946, 1952, and 1971 the Division of Christian Education of the National Council of the Churches of Christ in the United States of America. Used by permission. All rights reserved.

Scripture passages referencing the Septuagint LXX have been paraphrased from the YouVersion, specifically https://www.bible.com/bible/111/pro.17:14 and https://www.bible.com/bible/111/pro.18:19.

Scripture references marked as "TPT" are taken from The Holy Bible, the Passion Translation®. Copyright © 2017, 2018, 2020 by Passion & Fire Ministries, Inc. Used by permission. All rights reserved. ThePassionTranslation.com

Cover and Interior Layout by 2025 Harvest Creek Publishing and Design, www.harvestcreek.net
Cover Art by Garry Masterson

Ordering Information: Churches, associations, and others can receive discounts on quantity purchases. For details, please contact the author using the information listed at the back of the book.

Got Wisdom? Volume II—1st ed.

ISBN: 978-1-961641-35-8
Printed in the United States of America

CONTENTS

PRAISE FOR GOT WISDOM? Volume II..2

CONTENTS..7

HOW TO BENEFIT FROM THIS BOOK...13

ACKNOWLEDGMENTS...15

FOREWORD..17

Our Plans and God's Answer..19

The Lord Knows Our Spirits...24

Commitment..27

What Is Your Purpose?..30

Who Are Proud In Heart?...33

Forgiveness..37

Who Do You Want to Please?..40

The Righteous...44

The Lord Guides Us...48

A Good King...52

Get Wisdom 56

The Straight Road...59

Pride 62

Humility...65

Trust in the Lord 68

Our Speech..72

Gracious Words	75
Knowing Right	78
Work	82
Worthless People	86
A Crown of Glory	90
Controlling Our Anger	93
Rolling the Dice	97
Peace and Quiet	100
Serving Faithfully	103
The Crucible Refines Us	106
Evil Feeds on Evil	110
Do Not Mock the Poor	113
The Beauty of Family	116
Truth Can Be Trusted	120
The Bribe	123
True Friendship	126
Receptive or Resistant?	129
Rebellion	133
Never Return Evil for Good	136
Stop the Leak	140
Justice and Integrity	143
A Fool Has No Sense	147
A True Friend	150
Prudence and Promises	153

Build a Bridge, not a Wall	156
Our Heart's Condition	160
Fools Mess Up Life	164
Rejoice! Be Glad!	167
Greed	171
Wisdom Right in Front of You	174
The Pain Foolish Living Creates	177
Fair Judgment	180
A Cool Spirit	183
Be Open	187
The Closed-Minded Fool	190
Concern, Not Contempt	193
Deep and Refreshing	196
Not Good	199
A Fool's Mouth	202
A Sluggard's Ways	205
Where is Your Trust?	208
Haughty or Humble?	213
Listen, Listen	216
The Darkness of Depression	219
A Discerning Heart	223
Gift Giving	226
The Truth is the Issue	229
A Coin Toss	232

Guarding Good Relationships	234
The Power of Our Words	238
A Great Treasure	241
The Rich and the Poor	244
A True Friend	247
Integrity is Better	250
No Rush	254
Blaming God	257
Being a Friend	261
Be Truthful	264
Discovering Good	267
Jarring Absurdities	270
Living Big	273
Using Power for Good	276
Pain or Peace?	279
Lazybones	283
Keeping your life	287
Lending a hand	291
Good Guidance	294
Anger	299
Accepting Advice	302
God's Purpose	305
A Worthy Goal	308
The Fear of the Lord	311

The Poor Sluggard 316
A Scoffer 319
ABOUT THE AUTHORS 322
MEET THE CONTRIBUTORS 323
CONTACT INFORMATION 327

HOW TO BENEFIT FROM THIS BOOK

Got Wisdom? Volume II picks up where the first volume left off, continuing a social media discussion from early 2024. Almost daily, the digital conversation continued with posts reflecting on and offering insights from a specific scripture.

This book centers its discussions on Proverbs 16-19. Each commentary addresses one or two verses sequentially, but readers have two options to benefit from the dialogue. They may choose to read the devotions in numerical order, starting at the beginning of this book. Or they may decide to read them randomly, as the Lord leads. Space is provided at the end of each Commentary for readers to write about the insights they gained from the devotion.

In the Bible, wisdom is often presented as vital for a life that honors God and helps others. Proverbs 3:13-15 (NIV) describes the benefits to one who seeks wisdom. This book will assist in that effort.

Blessed are those who find wisdom,
those who gain understanding,
for she is more profitable than silver
And yields better returns than gold.
She is more precious than rubies;
Nothing you desire can compare with her.

ACKNOWLEDGMENTS

A sincere thank you to the contributors for these conversations:

*Barrett, Leslie, Cynthia, Kyle,
Frank H., Myra, Jim J., Kelley,
Cindy, Doreen, Jim, Frank,
Cindi, Frank C., Bruce,
Wright, John, and Cliff*

FOREWORD

AS SOMEONE WHO spends much of my time working with young adults—seminary students and their families who are preparing for a life in ministry—I see every day the deep hunger for wisdom. They're asking the big questions: How can I know God is calling me? How can I best prepare my life and heart to serve him? What does faithfulness to Jesus look like in the complexity of today's world?

In those moments, I often point them back to the wisdom found in the Word of God, which doesn't merely offer advice but speaks with God's living, active authority. The book of Proverbs, in particular, continues to surprise me with how timely and practical it is. It offers an enduring invitation to seek out the wisdom of God, who promises to respond: "Trust in the Lord with all your heart and lean not on your own understanding; in all your ways submit to him, and he will make your paths straight" (Proverbs 3:5–6). That promise isn't theoretical—I've watched God fulfill it repeatedly in the lives of those who turn to Him.

I remember (what seems not so long ago!) being in that same stage of life, full of questions and eager for clarity. One of the most formative voices during that season was a pastor I worked with named Garry Masterson. Garry and his wife Cindy welcomed me into their church in Fulshear, Texas, taking a chance on me as a young, untried leader to work with teenagers, including their two sons. Their influence showed me that a life and family dedicated to the Lord could be full of joy, grace, and grounded faith.

Garry didn't just teach wisdom—he embodied it, showing me what it looks like to love God and people with quiet faithfulness and deep joy. When I learned he had coauthored a book on wisdom from Proverbs with Ward Schmidt, a true wisdom-filled servant of Christ, I was thrilled—especially to hear that a second volume was coming. Being invited to write the foreword for this volume was a true gift. As I read through the material you're holding now, I encountered not just helpful insight, but also Spirit-breathed wisdom that spoke directly into my own life and walk with God.

This book is not only a meditation on Scripture—it's a conversation. Drawing from the voices of multiple conversation partners, it unfolds in a format that includes dialogue from social media. That might surprise some readers. After all, we don't often associate social media with wisdom. Our feeds are sometimes filled with quick takes, divisive opinions, and shallow noise.

But here, the format becomes part of the message. These conversations—sparked by Proverbs and shaped by humility, reflection, and a deep desire to follow God—model what it looks like to engage Scripture in community. I found myself nodding, pausing, even praying in response to what I read. In a world that often rewards being loud and reactive, this book creates space to slow down, reflect, and allow God's Word to speak. It also offers a hopeful vision for how technology can be used redemptively by Christians to build one another up rather than tearing each other down.

I was struck by how these reflections spoke into the very areas where I still long for God's guidance. It reminded me that wisdom isn't something we outgrow at any age or stage; it's something we return to again and again. This book invites readers not just to understand Proverbs, but to wrestle with its truths in the context of everyday life. It's both refreshment and challenge, calling us to listen more closely for God's voice and to walk more faithfully in His ways. This is wisdom that's not just learned—it's supposed to be lived.

So I encourage you: don't rush through these pages. Let them speak. Let them stir your questions, awaken your prayers, and remind you that God's wisdom is available, timely, and deeply personal. Let it guide you into dialogue with those around you who have wisdom from the Lord to offer from their own lives. Share the wisdom you gather here with others. And especially, may this book draw you nearer to the heart of the One who is Wisdom itself, and who gives wisdom generously to all who ask.

Rev. Dr. Jessica LaGrone
Seeker of Wisdom, Dean of Chapel, Asbury Theological Seminary

OUR PLANS AND GOD'S ANSWER

TODAY'S PASSAGE:

The plans of the heart belong to man, but the answer of the tongue is from the LORD.

Proverbs 16:1

COMMENTARY:

From Garry: As human beings, we make our plans, but in the final analysis, the Lord establishes our steps. That is because God is sovereign. God takes the thoughts and intentions of our hearts and directs them in ways that glorify Him. We don't really understand all that is in our hearts. We cannot clearly comprehend our own way, wisdom, or understanding. But the Lord is the sovereign God who has the final say in the matters of life.

Human beings can make plans, we can make choices, and we can set things up, but ultimately, God is in control. The Lord directs, oversees, and establishes as He sees fit. We formulate our hopes and dreams, but we also have certain limitations. The truth is that God is God. He has the final word. We can trust Him because God knows what is best. In the end, God's purpose stands.

From Ward: God is the source of all wisdom, truth, and life. We cannot know what is real and true without input from the Lord of the Universe. The tongue in this verse is the Word that the Lord speaks to us. His Word is the speech that gives direction, comfort, and peace. We make plans in our minds, and we see them accomplished because the Lord allows them to be. The better plans are the ones we make in accordance with the commands written in the Bible.

Many non-believers scoff at the concept that God speaks to humans. They see those who hear God as unintelligent or brain-damaged. Yet God speaks through reading the Bible, talking with friends, and sometimes as we pray. As He spoke into the darkness to create all that exists, He still speaks to both our darkened minds and to our open minds too. He talks to everyone who is alive, but few have open ears to listen. And fewer still even *want* to listen.

One of the first times I believed God was talking to me, He told me of His deep love for me. I hope every reader can know that same reality: that God really loves you and cares about your daily life. Despite the tragedies of this world, which God has not caused, He wants to walk with us each day. And we must acknowledge that He exists. Let none of us make our plans so complicated or self-centered that we cannot hear an answer from the Lord's mouth.

From Barrett: I believe He gave us free will because it is only in freedom that we can truly "spread our wings." By giving us this freedom, He hopes we will make choices that will put us on the righteous path that He has chosen for us. Indeed, we make our choices, but God ultimately guides our steps, whether they lead to salvation or ruin.

From Leslie: I totally agree with your thoughts. "Lord" here is Adonai (ruler/master). He is Master over everything!

From Cynthia: This Scripture holds several meanings for me. It has convicted me, and I have been protected from others' plans when I wasn't aware of danger. When my plans are deceitful, I ask for God's forgiveness. I pray for God's tongue to intervene on my behalf, as He's done in the past. I also pray for Him to prevent harm when I'm confused by circumstances beyond my understanding.

From Kyle: I must admit I struggle with this passage and with what most resources tell us it means. I read the following passage, taken directly from *Got Questions* online. This quote is found at https://www.gotquestions.org/Lord-directs-steps.html:

Solomon, in the book of Proverbs, discusses the relationship of man's planning and God's directing work multiple times (Proverbs 16:1; 19:21; 20:24). One example of this is found in Proverbs 16:9 (NJKV): "A man's heart plans his way, But the LORD directs his steps." Humanity often plans and prepares for future events, but in each case, God directs the outcome.

The book of Job provides a great example of this relationship between one's plans and God's directing ministry. God considered Job a righteous man (Job 1:1, 8). Undoubtedly, Job had plans, including continued work in the fields (Job 1:14–15), making sacrifices for his children (Job 1:5), accepting good from the Lord (Job 2:10), etc. During a prosperous time of Job's life (Job 1:1–3), Satan appeared before the Lord and was given permission to test Job's fear of the Lord. Satan carried out this testing by taking things that belonged to Job such as his material possessions, family, and health, sure that Job would curse God because of his loss. God directed these events, utilizing Satan as a tool for testing Job (Job 1:12; 2:6). Job certainly did not plan on losing all his possessions (Job 1:13–17), his children dying in a natural disaster (Job 1:18–19), and having his wife tell him to curse God and die (Job 2:9), but God directed the outcomes.

The story of Job doesn't end there, of course, but the contrast in Job's plans and the steps that God directed Job to take shows the relationship between man's future planning and God's present directing work. Just as God directed the circumstances and events in the life of Job, God directs and determines our circumstances and events today. We can take comfort in knowing that the Almighty God is in control of outcomes.

Another example of the Lord directing the steps of humanity is seen in Psalm 37:20–26. David, the second king of Israel, wrote this psalm in the later years of his life (Psalm 37:25). Part of the psalm contrasts the actions taken by the Lord toward the wicked and the righteous. In verse 22 David discusses "those the Lord blesses" and "those He curses." The blessed are the righteous under the Mosaic Law, while the cursed are the wicked (see Deuteronomy 27—28). The righteous man, who delights in the Lord, is promised "firm steps," (Psalm 37:23). He can move forward with confidence because, "though he may stumble, he will not fall, for the Lord upholds him with his hand," (verse 24).

> As a result of God's directing work, David rejoices in the outcomes: "Wrongdoers will be destroyed; the offspring of the wicked will perish. The righteous will inherit the land and dwell in it forever," (Psalm 37:28b–29). God's sovereignty should comfort the believer in Christ.

I see God's hand in our work and in the events and circumstances which shape our lives. However, this infringes on the theological concept of free will. Does God test us? Does God cause misfortune to see how I respond? Does God cause me to fail and others to succeed? Or does that happen because I did not follow God's plans, direction, counsel, or wisdom? There is a difference between God directing my steps and forcing my steps.

From Frank H.: Man proposes, but God disposes. Humans are made in God's image and have free will and the freedom to think and plan. God's ways, however, are not our ways, and our thoughts and plans sometimes don't fit into His purpose for us and others. It can be difficult, but when things don't go our way, we must remind ourselves that God is still in control. And that His plan is always perfect.

From Myra: Garry, congratulations on this newest endeavor. I'll share my thoughts on this proverb, but I looked beyond verse one:

> *The preparations of the heart belong to man, But the answer of the tongue is from the LORD. All the ways of a man are pure in his own eyes, But the LORD weighs the spirits. Commit your works to the LORD, And your thoughts will be established.*
>
> **Proverbs 16:1-3 (NKJV)**

Verses 2 and 3 help me understand the first verse. The Lord knows we will make plans, and that process belongs to us. But when we commit those plans to the Lord, then how we speak, act, and think will honor the Lord's will.

PRAYER:

Father, as I walk with You today, may I realize You oversee and guide my plans. I can trust Your wisdom and Your goodness today. Amen.

CHALLENGE:

As I seek to live a faithful life, I will trust God for my future.

_____
_____
_____
_____
_____
_____

THE LORD KNOWS OUR SPIRITS

 **TODAY'S PASSAGE:**

All the ways of a man are pure in his own eyes, but the Lord weighs the spirit.
Proverbs 16:2

COMMENTARY:

From Garry: We have the natural human tendency to love our own opinions. We think they are right. We tend to see only the best in ourselves, but God knows the truth. God knows our heart and soul, understands all the intricate details, and is aware of our motivations and intentions. God sees us perfectly, and we do not. Proverbs 12:15 (ESV) observes that it is the fool who views himself as right, but a "wise man listens to advice." We can trust God's assessment of us.

How can we see ourselves clearly and accurately? I am reminded of Hebrews 4:12b (ESV), which says God's Word is "sharper than any two-edged sword, piercing to the division of soul and spirit, of joints and marrow, and discerning the thoughts and intentions of the heart." The God to whom we are to give account sees clearly. The more we grow in our encounter with God and the Scriptures, the more we grow in our self-understanding.

From Ward: The writers of some posts on social media seem greatly concerned that the reader knows with certainty that their opinions are correct.

When we insist that what we see with our eyes is the only observation, we walk away from kindness and compassion. The need to be right reduces our ability to have close relationships with others. Our eyes are not the only ones that can see. The standard of purity is from the Lord, not from our thinking. This proverb tells us that the Lord knows our motives. I wonder if I always know the motive behind my words and thoughts.

How can we avoid thinking that our ways are always pure?

- First, we can ask ourselves what we can learn from others rather than what we must teach others.
- Second, we can ask ourselves if we are judging others rather than conversing with them.
- Last, we can refrain from assuming instant adversity when approaching a task or person and offer kindness and patience instead.

These are tough actions to take, but they are part of being the Lord's person.

From Jim J.: The human mind is a fickle thing. Even our imagination plays into deceiving ourselves. The more time I spend in prayer, Scripture, and contemplation, the more I see the need I have for God to guide me.

From Kelley: When we become full of ourselves, we become narcissistic, and that separates us from God. It is when we put the concerns of others ahead of our own that we truly show the love of God to this broken world. And that can be a true challenge. It is only with the help of the Lord Jesus that we can do this.

From Frank H.: Garry, I think that is a good discernment. God knows when I don't know what my intentions are; you're right. We are easily fooled.

From Leslie: Great word. We can do "good" things with bad motives. God sees our hearts. Psalm 139:23-24 (ESV) says, "Search me, O God, and know my heart! Try me and know my thoughts! And see if there be any grievous way in me, and lead me in the way everlasting!"

From Cindy: Luke 6:43-45 discusses the importance of what's in our heart, for it's out of our hearts that we speak. And God knows what's in our hearts, and He can change our hearts as well!

From Doreen: Humans tend to think they are good people. However, God looks at how we think, as well as how we speak, treat others, and so on. All that we do is visible to Him.

PRAYER:

Lord, thank You for knowing us better than we know ourselves. Help us trust You and follow Your lead. Amen.

CHALLENGE:

> *Trust in the Lord with all your heart and do not lean on your own understanding.*
>
> **Proverbs 3:5 (ESV)**

_____

_____

_____

_____

_____

_____

_____

COMMITMENT

 **TODAY'S PASSAGE:**

Commit your work to the LORD, and your plans will be established.
                                                           Proverbs 16:3

COMMENTARY:

From Garry: When our lives are committed to the Lord, we can count on the promise Jesus made from the Sermon on the Mount. He made it clear that if we follow through in putting His teaching into practice, we will be like a wise man—one who built his life upon a rock-solid foundation.

The word *commit* in its original sense, conveys the image of rolling our work onto the Lord. We are to cast our burdens upon the Lord; we are to place all that we do in His hands. It portrays complete dependence on Him.

When I walk by faith and live humbly before God, I can trust God to take care of me and use me for His kingdom. In other words, as I share my life with God, I can trust that God will establish it in a way that brings Him glory.

From Ward: "My way or the highway" is a popular notion today. But this proverb does not state that. A good outcome for any project does not come just from our own intelligence, insight, labor, or tools but must have input from God. I wonder how many people in the Universe even see this as a possibility. How do we commit our work to the Lord? The answer is more than just saying aloud a sentence. Commitment to God means following the instructions that His people have written in the Bible. One location is found in Romans 12:9-18. Some of these directions include:

- being sincere
- regarding what is good

- honoring one another
- working diligently
- praying continually
- not thinking you know everything
- not avenging yourself
- trying to live at peace with each other

Wow, what a great list! If everyone in the world did just one of these actions, our environment would be more godly. Rather than thinking about what others could do, I am going to focus on fulfilling these requirements. That is the way for my plans to be established and for me to bring God's life into this world.

From Frank H.: Offer up your work and all you do each day to the glory of God. Your work and day will be better for it.

From Barrett: The many promises of the Lord in the Bible are not conditional, are they? In most cases, He promised "I will do this" or "I will make this happen" with no conditions. He said, "So you will be my people, and I will be your God," (Jeremiah 30:22 [NIV]). Committing to the Lord confirms you are one of His people. His promise makes Him your God. Make your way firmly in righteousness, and your soul will be blessed by the promise. God is steadfast; there can be no other way.

From Leslie: Great word!! Ecclesiastes 9:10a (NIV) says, "Whatever your hand finds to do, do it with all your might." When we commit our work to the Lord, it changes our perspective and our attitude.

From Jim J.: True—and I needed to remember this after a rough week.

From Doreen: Years ago, I was watching a minister on TV, and he said, "If you don't know what your passion is, pray for God to reveal it to you." After hearing this, God answered my prayer and showed me how to naturally heal my eczema. This led me on a path to my current career as a wellness and nutrition advisor.

Every day, as I work for God, I pray for Him to give me the wisdom to know how to help my customers and for discernment to know what to say to them. I also ask Him to give me credibility with my customers. Additionally, I include some of them on my prayer list when they are ill.

This practice has been extremely helpful to me. I can't tell you how often people tell me they feel as though God led them to talk to me. Many times, I am able to provide answers to what they are seeking in prayer. These answers are often confirmed by other people or through the written word.

PRAYER:

Lord, this is a day You have made. May I live for Your glory and trust You. Amen.

CHALLENGE:

Give your work to God today. Live for Him, and He will take it from there. Watch what He will do.

_____
_____
_____
_____
_____
_____

WHAT IS YOUR PURPOSE?

TODAY'S PASSAGE:

> *The LORD has made everything for its purpose, even the wicked for the day of trouble.*
>
> **Proverbs 16:4**

COMMENTARY:

From Garry: God is sovereign. There are no loose ends in God's creation. Everything will be put to some use and matched with its proper outcome. This does not mean that God is the author of evil. Rather, God has the final word. God has made the world with a moral order. Right and wrong, truth and lies, good and evil all exist. And there *are* consequences to our actions. God alone is the judge over all. The final chapter in Ecclesiastes states that the ultimate conclusion involves fearing God and keeping His commandments. This is the whole duty of humanity. "God will bring every deed into judgment, with every secret thing, whether good or evil," (Ecc. 12:14 [ESV]).

From Ward: When I get depressed, I think my life has no purpose. When I can pull out of any depression, life seems to have meaning. Experiencing severe trauma can allow a person to see all life as capricious, painful, and without focus. The Lord wants us to believe that He has established a purpose for all pieces of the universe that have been created, both living and non-living. Wow, even the rocks and the clouds have meaning. The general purpose of living is to give praise and glory to God. Yet, all people have a specific purpose in life that is unique to them. This is more than a job or a role in a family.

Here is an assignment. Take a moment and think of a purpose or purposes you have had or have now. What are they? Write them down on this page. Next, how do you fulfill or do your purpose(s)? I wonder if some readers are having difficulty thinking of words to write.

The Milewalk Academy suggests these four actions: Sacrifice, Learn, Believe, and Focus–not bad advice. Does the Bible have any similar words? Yes, in 1 Peter 1:5, the Bible lists several actions we can all do to bring success to our tasks. One of the words is "virtue," or the Greek word *arete*, which translates to virtue or goodness, meaning to fulfill one's purpose or function. Therefore, the writer of 2 Peter believes that as we exercise virtue and godly goodness, we can attain our ultimate purpose.

If you need help remembering what character traits are godly, please refer to Galatians 5:22-23, which lists the fruits of the Spirit. We can trust that acting godly in all situations and tasks will help fulfill our purpose in living. May all who read this find meaning when doing godly goodness.

From Doreen: Being an avid hiker, I see that God's creation is perfect and everything was created to keep the world in perfect harmony. Throughout my life, I have come to realize all things work together for the good of those who love God.

Everyone has free will, but we all make poor choices. Some people have more pain in their lives, and they make worse choices than other people. I know that evil does not come from God; I also know that hurting people hurt other people.

Some of my poor choices have turned out better than I expected. Unpleasant experiences have allowed me to help others. In addition, the pain inflicted on me by others has taught me more about the importance of forgiveness.

I've also learned to praise God in the midst of the storm. Sometimes, it's hard, but I know He is watching over me and taking care of me.

From Jim: This is challenging and very thought-provoking. It took me somewhere I do not often go. Thank you for this one.

PRAYER:

O God, You alone are the sovereign God over all. All creation is accountable to You. May I live in that awareness, trusting in Your goodness and grace. Amen.

CHALLENGE:

Know that everything you say or do is heard and seen by a sovereign Lord, and God holds you accountable for your actions.

_____
_____
_____
_____
_____
_____
_____

WHO ARE PROUD IN HEART?

TODAY'S PASSAGE:

Everyone who is arrogant in heart is an abomination to the LORD; be assured, he will not go unpunished.

Proverbs 16:5

COMMENTARY:

From Garry: Arrogance reveals an exaggerated sense of one's own importance. This kind of pride causes a person to show disdain. This attitude of pride creates tension and strife. It opposes the fear of the Lord. It exalts itself. Arrogance prevents our love of God and neighbor. That is why God cannot tolerate pride in our hearts.

The word "arrogant" originates from a root word meaning "locust," referring to a swarm that devours all the crops. This kind of pride is like a locust swarm that always hinders a true spiritual harvest within us. Pride trips us up.

An image that comes to my mind is the story about the Pharisee and the tax collector. The Pharisee expresses pride in his prayer, thanking God for all his own good works and for being unlike the tax collector. However, the tax collector humbles himself and cries out for mercy. Watch out for pride—God cannot stand it because it blinds us and trips us up.

From Ward: Being "arrogant in heart" means having arrogance in your mind, even if your actions do not show this. God is concerned about what we think, as well as what we do with our hands and our voices. I do not know how to see conceit inside a person's mind. But God can. He wants this to be ridden from our minds, and if not, we can expect discipline. Generally, the proud and haughty are taken down by their own swagger. As they persist in their self-importance, they will make mistakes and offend others. These errors and unkind words will bring defeat to their plans and work.

Yet our culture honors those who are independent, self-reliant, forceful, and pushing through to the end, no matter who is hurt along the way. Those who are humble and who look for wise counsel from the community are not honored or exalted. I often wonder, *how many business failures happen because of the arrogance of the owners?* The leaders of past empires were conceited and boastful, and where are their empires now?

Humble Jesus still receives the adulation of billions today. There is a lesson here that forsaking arrogance will lead to a more peaceful outcome than grasping conceit. May all of us seek to do what Philippians 2:3b (NKJV) says, "In lowliness of mind let each esteem others better than himself."

From Frank: Pride goes before the fall, and those arrogant in heart may be susceptible to believing they are their own god. Watch out that you do not deceive yourself.

From Barrett: Ecclesiastes says that the end of the matter involves fearing God and keeping His commandments. Honestly, I struggle with the concepts of 'fearing God' and 'God-fearing people' ideas. What do we have to fear in God? He formed us in His image. We are part of Him. He is part of us. He loves us as a father and creator and has a plan for us. We can fear our sins and transgressions. We can fear His awesome power and His judgment.

But if we keep His commandments, if we believe His Son Jesus Christ died for our sins and rose again to defeat death as our Savior so that we may receive the gift of eternal life, should we fear God?

- John 1:12-13 (NIV) says, "Yet to all who did receive him, to those who believed in his name, he gave the right to become children of God—children born not of natural descent, nor of human decision or a husband's will, but born of God."
- John 5:24 (NIV) says, "Very truly I tell you, whoever hears my word and believes him who sent me has eternal life and will not be judged but has crossed over from death to life."
- John 11: 25-26a (NIV) says, "Jesus said to her, 'I am the resurrection and the life. The one who believes in me will live, even though they die; and whoever lives by believing in me will never die.'"

- John 20:30-31 (ESV) says, "Now Jesus did many other signs in the presence of the disciples, which are not written in this book; but these are written so that you may believe that Jesus is the Christ, the Son of God, and that by believing you may have life in his name."
- 1 Timothy 1:16 (NIV) says, "But for that very reason I was shown mercy so that in me, the worst of sinners, Christ Jesus might display his immense patience as an example for those who would believe in him and receive eternal life."

From Myra: Boasting is addressed often in God's Word. This scripture from Jeremiah 9 says so much to us:

> *Thus says the LORD: "Let not the wise man boast in his wisdom, let not the mighty man boast in his might, let not the rich man **boast** in his riches, but let him who boasts **boast** in this, that he understands and knows me, that I am the LORD who practices steadfast love, justice, and righteousness in the earth. For in these things, I delight, declares the LORD."*
> **Jeremiah 9:23-24 (ESV, Emphasis Added)**

The Apostle Paul speaks of boasting in his letters to the churches in Rome, Corinth, Galatia, Ephesus, and Thessalonica:

- "May I never **boast** except in the cross of our Lord Jesus Christ...." (Galatians 6:14a [NIV, Emphasis Added]).
- "For by grace you have been saved through faith; and this is not your own doing, it is the gift of God—not because of works, lest any man should ***boast***. For we are his workmanship, created in Christ Jesus for good works, which God prepared beforehand, that we should walk in them," (Ephesians 2:8-10 [RSV, Emphasis Added]).

PRAYER:

Lord, may I not exalt myself today. May I exalt You and humbly serve in Your Name. Amen.

CHALLENGE:

Do not think of yourself more highly than you ought to think, but view yourself honestly.

_____
_____
_____
_____
_____
_____
_____

FORGIVENESS

🌳 TODAY'S PASSAGE:

> *By steadfast love and faithfulness iniquity is atoned for, and by fear of the LORD one turns away from evil.*
>
> **Proverbs 16:6**

COMMENTARY:

From Garry: As I looked over various Bible translations of today's passage, I noticed these phrases:

- "Through loyal love and truth," (Proverbs 16:6 [NET])
- "By mercy and lovingkindness," (Proverbs 16:6 [AMP])
- "If we truly love God…show him respect," (Proverbs 16:6 [CEV])

I thought about the path we walk through faith. It is a journey of holiness. It is a process of learning and growing. Each day, we can go to God and experience His forgiveness when we sin. Sometimes, we continue to commit a particular sin repeatedly. Still, God continues to forgive us through Jesus Christ's work on the cross.

Over time, we commit that sin less and less. We grow in holiness. It takes time. God is patient with us. He knows and understands our weaknesses. God does not give up on us. I really like how the Passion Translation puts it: "You can avoid evil through surrendered worship and the fear of God, for the power of his faithful love removes sin's guilt and grip over you," (Proverbs 16:6 [TPT]).

From Ward: Atone means to cover. The instructions for the Hebrews in Leviticus 4 say animals can be killed as a sacrifice. Their blood would atone for or cover the sins of the people, and their sins would be forgiven. In the same way, Jesus was killed on the cross, and his blood atoned for the sins of people who believed. And God forgives their sin.

We can also cover the sins of those we know and provide forgiveness to them. We cover the sins of others not through a sacrifice of blood, but by offering love, kindness, faithfulness, and mercy. We should not broadcast or gossip about the sins of others, but be willing to provide forgiveness and offer comfort. This does not happen much on social media now. Exposing the sins of those we dislike and exaggerating the effects of their actions does not bring peace to the world.

Additionally, for centuries, people on our planet have lost any fear of God. We fear others, the economy, the future, or natural disasters, and have no thought about God. As a result, evil flourishes. How do we stop evil in our midst? For the community to fear God rather than other people. Let us pray that our world changes so that all its residents may fearfully respect God.

From Leslie: The Complete Jewish Bible says, "Grace and truth atone for iniquity, and people turn from evil through fear of ADONAI" (Proverbs 16:6 [CJB]). This reminds me of the truth from John:

> *And the Word became flesh and dwelt among us, and we beheld his glory, the glory as of the only begotten of the Father [the One and Only], full of grace and truth [Emphasis Added]. Jesus is grace and truth. We must trust Him alone for our salvation because He is the One who atoned for our sin.*
> **John 1:14 (NKJV)**

From Jim: Garry, thank you for this one. As I worked on my exegetical analysis for chapter 9 in Genesis, God's commitment and love truly are amazing. And your words resonated with my experience all these years of walking with God.

From Doreen: I appreciate the reminder in this passage that God will continue to forgive us and help us turn away from sins and bad habits.

PRAYER:

Lord, thank You for Your constant and faithful love and mercy. May I learn to live in Your love and grow in godly living through Your amazing grace. Amen.

CHALLENGE:

Accept God's full mercy in Christ. Take the next step in living by faith.

_____
_____
_____
_____
_____
_____
_____

WHO DO YOU WANT TO PLEASE?

 **TODAY'S PASSAGE:**

When a man's ways please the LORD, he makes even his enemies to be at peace with him.

Proverbs 16:7

COMMENTARY:

From Garry: Think about it. What does a person's life look like that pleases the Lord? A description that comes to my mind is a person who is secure, self-controlled, and approachable. A person who pleases the Lord embraces God and His ways of peace. They offer respect to others, which has a disarming effect, bringing peace instead of war and respect instead of regret.

Live for the audience of "One." Consult God's wishes, not man's; God can handle the people you fear. Be a God-pleaser. Proverbs 29:25 (MSG) says, "The fear of human opinion disables; trusting in GOD protects you from that."

From Ward: 2 Corinthians 5:9b (ESV) says, "We make it our aim to please him [God]." How can we please God? Hebrews 11 says, "And without faith, it is impossible to please him [God]," (Hebrews 11:6a [ESV, Emphasis Added]). We please God when we have faith in Him. Faith is more than a statement of what we believe; it is an ongoing, daily relationship with the Lord. When our actions align with what we know is true about God, we demonstrate that we have a positive relationship with Him. Our daily thoughts and actions should follow the instructions God's people have written in the Bible. These activities are more than memorizing the Ten Commandments in Exodus 20.

Where are the lists of actions we can do that come from our faith relationship with God? Philippians 4:8, I Thessalonians 5:11-22, Romans 12:9-21, and Titus 2:1-10 contain great words for all of us to follow. Having these attributes leads to godliness in our lives. And godly living produces peace. As Isaiah 32:17a (ESV) says, "And the effect of righteousness will be peace."

Additionally, this proverb states a principle that even peace with our enemies is possible when we focus on pleasing the Lord. Do we want peace in the world, peace at work, peace in our relationships? Then we walk righteously, work to establish justice, and peace will come. This is not a hope, a dream, or a guess. This is a promise from God to us, his people. May all of us make our aim to please God and not just ourselves.

From Leslie: It reminds me of the truth of Psalm 23. The Lord, as our Shepherd, prepares a table before us in the presence of our enemies. We can eat and be at rest in the presence of our enemies when God is our rock and our fortress.

From Frank: When we live our lives as God would have us live, our lives are more peaceful and filled. We even find peace in difficult relationships.

From Cindi: I have learned the hard way that there is no peace if you live to please others more than God! I ask God every morning to show me His will, and I intentionally place my day in His hands. In prayer, God will reveal to us our heart's motives, and in fellowship with Jesus, we will be corrected and redirected.

From Jim: The book of Proverbs offers many redemptive glimpses into the New Testament; therefore, its interpretation must always be framed in this light. Otherwise, they are simply wise sayings that even non-Christians could follow. With that in mind, I have two thoughts:

- First, consider Paul's prayer in Colossians: "[being] filled with the knowledge of his will in all spiritual wisdom and understanding," (Colossians 1:9b [ESV, Emphasis Added]). This leads to our walking in a manner worthy of the Lord and pleasing Him in all respects, "bearing fruit in every good work and increasing in the knowledge of God," (Colossians 1:10b [ESV]).

- Second, consider that our Lord was perfect in ALL that He did, yet had LOTS of enemies—so many that He was crucified. Therefore, we can't take one verse from Proverbs without considering the other verses and spiritual thoughts that may provide more context.

From Doreen: I am proof that Proverbs 16:7 is true. A few years ago, I decided to get up earlier to have time for my Bible study before work or any other commitments. I have a manager who is difficult to be around. She has made me and other coworkers cry, and they have been hesitant to approach her. However, her position as my supervisor demanded my respect. I worked on being more respectful toward her and began praying for her and for myself to find favor in her eyes. Now, she has changed her attitude towards me, and I have surely found favor with her.

From Cynthia: I thank God for not giving me everything I have ever asked for, especially when I neglect to reach out to God first. Music, but especially sacred music, has blessed me with knowledge of the ages, bringing Truth to my soul. I've always been curious about my ancestors, and I feel closest to past and present people when connecting through hymns. When we learn to take ourselves less seriously and let go of self-righteousness, we are led to pray for our enemies and any baffling circumstances. My desire is to point joyfully the way to Jesus.

From Jim: Deep and daring, a great question to explore about who runs my life.

PRAYER:

Lord, I love You. You are the strength of my life. Help me put You first in all I do or say today. Amen.

CHALLENGE:

Why do you do the things you do? Is it to please God or please yourself? Who sets the agenda in your life? Is it God or others?

_____
_____
_____
_____
_____
_____
_____

THE RIGHTEOUS

 **TODAY'S PASSAGE:**

> *Better is a little with righteousness than great revenues with injustice.*
> **Proverbs 16:8**

COMMENTARY:

From Garry: Today's passage is like Proverbs 15:16 (ESV): "Better is a little with the fear of the LORD than great treasure and trouble with it." It is not how much you have but how much you reflect the character of God. What really matters is living with integrity.

Proverbs 16:8 (MSG) from The Message Bible says: "Far better to be right and poor than to be wrong and rich." When I think about this proverb, a verse in the New Testament comes to mind: "But godliness with contentment is great gain, for we brought nothing into the world, and we cannot take anything out of the world. But if we have food and clothing, with these we will be content"(1 Timothy 6:6-8 [ESV]).

The primary word in Proverbs 15:16 is "righteousness." Righteous thinking, righteous living, and righteous dealings that are fair and just are what really matter.
G. Wright Doyle, a friend of mine, wrote a book entitled *Worship and Wisdom*. He reflects on this verse:

> *When we gain at the expense of others, we incur their anger and envy... God has created us to love, not to lust; to give, not to get; to deny ourselves, not to destroy others. In His time, He will reward all righteous deeds.*
> **G. Wright Doyle**

From Ward: How much is enough? Is it the same for all people in the same nation? In the news feed I receive each time I get on my internet browser, there is at least one article about how much money to save for a comfortable retirement. And the amount always seems way more than most people can hope to save during their working years. I guess that these articles probably produce anxiety, hopelessness, and sadness for some readers. This proverb tells us not to steal, manipulate, or lie to gain wealth. Whatever possessions and money we have that were earned with dignity, integrity, and hard work are better than defrauding others to gain more dollar bills in our bank account.

When I was younger, I envied those who, through illegal or shady acts, obtained many possessions, while those who were righteous appeared to have much less. How could this result be "better?" In our world today, the definition of success is the person who ends up with the most toys, the most chips, the most points, or the most dollar bills.

In God's economy, the winners are those who are faithful to his rules. Often, being faithful to God means we have fewer possessions, less money in the bank, more persecution, and less recognition from the world. This world is not our home. We are just passing by. The earth is just one stop on the road to eternal life. As we focus on being a child of God, we can relieve ourselves of the stress of continually striving to gain more. Lord, help us be content and comfortable with Your provision for us and our families.

From Cindi: As I enter "old age," I realize how little I care about material possessions. I am constantly looking for ways to simplify my life. Things I once thought were very important have been sent to the garbage bin or given to charity if reusable. As I walk with Jesus through this latter part of life, I see that real relationships and knowing God are most important and fulfilling.

From Doreen: I've learned that gratitude, even in hard times, brings blessings, though not always large ones. Sometimes, it's a tiny thing that means a lot. Other times, it's a BIG blessing that I have been praying for. I know that cheating on my way to success won't feel comfortable.

From Frank C.: Amen! Well said!

From Cynthia: This message would have benefited my younger self. I thought I wasn't of the world, because I didn't like the current popular songs on the radio. Still, I was affected by the world of "wise buys," "sales," "birthday celebrations," and "extras—just in case." Many purchases were not bought with prayer or thought. Now, we live in an overstuffed world—where we tithe to our creditors, fill landfills, and mock our Savior's Power. Jesus gave everything—and yet there is no jewelry or furniture passed down from His death on the cross. I was convicted, so I believed it was important to have the security of an education, a job, a roof over my family's heads, and clothes.

Still, I didn't diligently seek ways to lead my family to Christ. I was busy in the church doing what I wanted to do and, therefore, what I thought God wanted me to do. Leading a simple life is part of being a great witness, and I'm grateful for those in my life who have built and maintained relationships through meaningful connections and hard work.

Dallas Willard, one of my favorite authors, had furniture worse than most of his visitors. But he purchased the house next door to keep his overflowing library of theological books.

From Jim: I thought on this one throughout Sunday, and how complicated life can easily get.

From Frank H.: As the Word says in Mark 8:36 (NIV), "What good is it for someone to gain the whole world, yet forfeit their soul?"

PRAYER:

Lord, thank You for all the ways You provide for me. May I use my possessions in a way that honors You and reflects justice. Amen.

CHALLENGE:

There is joy in simplicity.

_____
_____
_____
_____
_____
_____
_____

THE LORD GUIDES US

 **TODAY'S PASSAGE:**

The heart of man plans his way, but the LORD establishes his steps.
                                                            Proverbs 16:9

COMMENTARY:

From Garry: When you examine verses one, three, and nine of Proverbs 16 closely, you notice they are all very similar. They all deal with plans, and they all deal with God's sovereignty. On the human side, we are to make plans, commit those plans to God, and chart our course accordingly. We trust God will have the final say, grant success, and guide us every step of the way. There is a balance between human plans and God's oversight of the outcome. We can trust God as we make decisions that are faithful to God.

Duke theologian and bible scholar Ellen F. Davis wrote in her commentary on Proverbs:

> *A woman at a key juncture in her life exclaimed in frustration to her spiritual director, a nun of much experience and wisdom: "I'm forty years old, and I don't know whether I want to get married or be a nun!"*
>
> *The nun replied, "It doesn't matter."*
>
> *"What do you mean, it doesn't matter? Doesn't God have an opinion?"*
>
> *"No. What God cares about is that you live faithfully and give yourself fully, whichever path you choose. You are free to decide, and you must decide. You must go through the pain of decision to give yourself fully."*

From Ward: Early in our marriage, my wife and I went to a couple's seminar. We learned that both of us were excellent planners. We enjoy preparation, and this is one area we have in common. We even enjoy implementing the plans we have made. I wonder if other couples have the same experience. I know that many individuals enjoy making plans alone. I have not stayed in contact with many people to know if their plans ever produce a successful event. This proverb reminds the faithful follower of God that to have a good outcome for our plans, the Lord must help establish the steps of the idea.

How does the Lord do this? When we become reflections of His character in our planning. Integrity is important. As Titus 1:16a (NKJV) says, we should not "profess to know God, but in works they deny *Him*." When we plan, our character should reflect godly qualities. Titus 2:2, 6-8 tells us we should be sober, reverent, patient, and not corruptible with sound speech so that no one will condemn us.

If these aspects are seen by others, we can know that God will establish our plans. This does not mean our proposal will be accomplished, but we can have peace knowing that we were guided by godly principles in our design, regardless of the outcome.

From Bruce: I have a playground theory, which I realized many years ago. Playgrounds usually have boundaries or fences to keep children safe from outside interference and to keep children from running outside the boundaries and getting hurt. When we allow our children to play in the playground, we don't really care what equipment they play on as long as they stay within the boundaries.

I think that is the way God is—He doesn't care what equipment we play on as long as we stay within the boundaries of His grace, love, and care. And whatever we do, we do it heartily as unto the Lord.

From Cynthia: It's interesting that we reflect on this verse during the election season. Sometimes, we don't have worthy plans. It's in our best interest to pray for our leaders' steps, as well as our steps. When we are lost, God's Word is a lamp unto our feet. I want God to make my path straight without too much pain. We aren't God, and therefore, we waste valuable time agonizing over every decision. The past is gone. Everyone in the Bible made mistakes, except for Jesus. God is a master at planning.

From Myra: There is a lot of wisdom in this commentary. The pain of decision-making hits home. Thank you.

From Leslie: Good word.

From Frank C.: Wow! That's a great reflection and a wonderful truth from Ellen Davis, Garry, and the Lord.

From Doreen: I typically start my day with quiet time, studying, and prayer. If I must work, I pray for God to guide me in knowing what to say to help my customers. If we're going on a trip, I pray for God to keep us safe and to protect our bodies from injury and our vehicles from damage.

Once, on a trip, I traveled an hour, going the wrong way. I immediately told my family that we may never know what God was saving us from. I also enjoyed the beautiful route we took to get back on course. There had just been a weird change in our driving instructions that had led us astray. I call it a "divine mistake." Ultimately, I know that God has great plans for me in this journey of life.

From Jim: Wow, there is always much growth in wrestling to decide.

PRAYER:

Lord, thank You that I can trust You as I seek to honor You with my decisions. Please help me be faithful in the plans I make. Amen.

CHALLENGE:

Cooperate with God's guidance through His Word. Make your plans, trusting that God will guide and oversee things for His glory.

_____
_____
_____
_____
_____
_____
_____

A GOOD KING

 **TODAY'S PASSAGE:**

An oracle is on the lips of a king; his mouth does not sin in judgment. A just balance and scales are the LORD'S; all the weights in the bag are his work. It is an abomination to kings to do evil, for the throne is established by righteousness. Righteous lips are the delight of a king, and he loves him who speaks what is right. A king's wrath is a messenger of death, and a wise man will appease it. In the light of a king's face there is life, and his favor is like the clouds that bring the spring rain.

Proverbs 16:10-15

COMMENTARY:

From Garry: This cluster of verses pertains to the influence and authority of leaders. The king should proclaim what is true and right. A good king motivates and does not mislead or exploit. A king is supposed to promote justice and honesty in his business affairs. The law required that scales and balances be accurate.

The authority to rule with wisdom requires justice. Justice makes a government strong and secure. Good leaders build on a moral foundation, loving what is right and cultivating truthful speech.

Those in authority have power, so it is wise to know how to respond to their power. Good leaders possess the ability to show favor. The Message Bible paraphrases Proverbs 16:15 (MSG), "Good-tempered leaders invigorate lives; they're like spring rain and sunshine." Proverbs 14:34 (ESV) says: "Righteousness exalts a nation, but sin is a reproach to any people."

From Ward: Meeting a king personally is something I have never experienced—nor a queen, a prince, or a princess. I do not know how to talk to or act with a person of such standing. I guess I should be polite, not interrupt, not joke too much, and speak clearly. Yet that way of relating sounds like a pattern for talking to everyone new I meet.

Our culture would be different if we all treated each other like being with a king or queen. We could offer respect, be patient, and think before we speak. A royal leader is a person who ideally knows wisdom from falsehood, can decide righteously, and supervises his subjects with equity. Alas, too many leaders in our world have no training in how to lead, manage, and inspire followers. And too many followers distrust, lie to, and betray their leaders. How do we get out of this mess?

- Philippians 3:20a (NIV) says, "But our citizenship is in heaven." Humility is a virtue, even if most people have forgotten this.
- Colossians 4:1b (NIV) reminds that we "also have a Master in heaven."
- Philippians 2:3b (NIV) says, "In humility value others above yourselves."

Kings and subjects must realize that their decisions can profoundly affect many lives, and they have a responsibility to conduct themselves in a godly manner in their thoughts and actions. Let us all pray that each leader in business, government, faith, and family behaves with kindness and integrity toward all who follow.

From Leslie: Jesus is our King, and perhaps this is Solomon's foretelling of the One true King to come. I like your prayer, but I would add that all Believers also uphold truth and integrity. Please do not pass on things that are not true to advance your candidate. Our true hope is in the One.

From Cindi: There is so much anxiety and untruth surrounding political discourse today! All I know to do is pray for our nation and remember God is on the throne. It's going to be okay. It is good to hear the wisdom of Scripture to filter out all the noise.

From Barrett: This quote seems appropriate:

> *The brand of the anarchist is not logic but envy-driven power: to take it, to keep it, and to use it against purported enemies—which would otherwise be impossible in times of calm, or through the ballot box.*
> **Victor D. Hansen**

From Frank C.: Amen!

From Doreen: This is a valuable passage and offers excellent advice for individuals in leadership roles. I've seen great leaders who were patient and had great relationships with the people they oversaw. I've also seen leaders who were impatient, showed favoritism, and were intimidating. God expects more from the people in leadership roles.

From Cynthia: I'm concerned about America and the fear that an election can bring. Regardless of who is in office, our role is clear: to pray for our leaders. Love casts out all fear, and God is Love. Love God, and then we will love people. Praying for our leaders and ministers is so important, and we are confident that the government is on His shoulders.

PRAYER:

Lord, guide our nation. In this current political climate, we need a breath of fresh air. Bless our leaders to be people of integrity and truth who seek justice and righteousness. Amen.

CHALLENGE:

Pray for the Lord to guide the election of our next president.

_____
_____

GET WISDOM

 **TODAY'S PASSAGE:**

> *How much better to get wisdom than gold! To get understanding is to be chosen rather than silver.*
>
> **Proverbs 16:16**

COMMENTARY:

From Garry: Wisdom is so much more than knowledge. Wisdom is living God's way, which involves our interactions with people and our behavior. It is a prayer-filled life that is a channel of God's grace, reflecting the goodness of God. It does not come naturally, but it is a gift of God that we are to constantly seek as we walk with the Lord by faith. James 1 says:

> *If any of you lacks wisdom, let him ask God, who gives generously to all without reproach, and it will be given him. But let him ask in faith, with no doubting, for the one who doubts is like a wave of the sea that is driven and tossed by the wind.*
>
> **James 1:5-6 (ESV)**

Wisdom involves living a faithful life, one that depends on the Lord. And this lifestyle is far more valuable than a large bank account. The Message Bible puts Proverbs 16:16 (MSG) this way: "Get wisdom—it's worth more than money; choose insight over income every time."

From Ward: I wonder when the last time I had a wise thought. I value wisdom, but I sometimes think what I really focus on is my opinions. I have opinions and ideas about many people, events, and tasks. And a few judgments as well. How can I bring wisdom to my mind from my experiences? Here are some thoughts:

- Wisdom certainly comes from thinking about our life experiences. So, to gain wisdom, we must rub shoulders with other people. And with other people who may disagree with us. If I only talk with people who agree with me, then I believe all I have obtained is a popular opinion. I must know what I believe and why, as well as what I do not believe and why. This requires time for reflection. Sometimes, I must realize that I may have made a mistake and that I might need to adjust my thoughts.
- Wisdom involves thinking about universal truths that apply to all times and circumstances. Our observations of current affairs may lead to expert opinions but no wisdom. I want to be wise, but I first must be loving and compassionate. I do not think I have ever met an extremely angry, wise person.
- Wisdom develops over time when loving friends can be together, helping each other with the obstacles of living. I want that type of life. And I hope you can have that as well.

From Doreen: This is one of my favorite passages in Proverbs. Praying for wisdom has changed my life in so many ways. My mom has dementia and lives in a nursing home. I prayed for God to give me wisdom through what I was experiencing with her. As a result, I have changed my lifestyle because of the information and the wisdom I have gained from my research about dementia. I'm so much healthier now than I was five years ago.

From Cynthia: It may appear that I'm taking the scripture out of context, but sometimes I feel tossed by the sea regarding finances. And that may be the moment I should ask for wisdom. For example, just when I think the budget is good, unexpected bills come up. These situations allow me to thank God for the children who take care of me and that my home is paid off.

PRAYER:

Lord, thank You for freely offering wisdom every day. Your love and power are available to me as I simply come to You in faith, empowered by Your Holy Spirit. Amen.

CHALLENGE:

Seek wisdom! It is the best way to live!

_____
_____
_____
_____
_____
_____
_____

THE STRAIGHT ROAD

 **TODAY'S PASSAGE:**

The highway of the upright turns aside from evil; whoever guards his way preserves his life.

Proverbs 16:17

COMMENTARY:

From Garry: As we travel down the path of right living, we are intentional about avoiding wrong turns. We look ahead and are aware of those things that lead us astray. We maintain the right course, using discretion and understanding to stay on track. We keep our focus on Christ.

There are side roads that are hazardous. They may look harmless, but be careful because they could lead to trouble. If you get off track, make a U-turn and head back in the right direction. You will be glad you did. Traveling by faith is the best way to travel. The benefits are worth it.

Proverbs 11:3 (ESV) says, "The integrity of the upright guides them, but the crookedness of the treacherous destroys them." I am also reminded of Paul's exhortation in Romans 12:9 (ESV): "Let love be genuine. Abhor what is evil; hold fast to what is good."

From Ward: Guardrails and fences protect us. They provide limits for us and keep harmful elements away. This will preserve our lives. There is a story, maybe apocryphal, from a time in the last century. A school district decided that fences on the play areas made the school seem like a prison. So, the fences were removed. At playtime, the students were confused. Instead of filling the play yard with their presence, they all stayed close to the building because they did not know where the boundary was. The fence was later restored, and the students enjoyed the entire play area.

Providing limits and curbs for our actions and thoughts will keep us alive. We have a culture that supports a life where the only check is what we can imagine in our minds, along with the principle that we do not hurt anyone. A life as if we all lived in an individual glass bowl, and none of our actions affect anyone else. Rules are available to allow us to enjoy life, not to limit our fun. Turning from evil removes anxiety and dissatisfaction. I wish all the people of this world could understand that pursuing unhinged life experiences leads to distress and eventual emptiness. May our devotion to God and to limits bring us a peaceful life.

From Leslie: Yes, Lord, guard our hearts and minds in Christ Jesus.

From Cindi: When my husband Pat and I travel by car, I feel like I need a hard copy of a map to help guide us. Yes, I know I can download directions, and cars have GPS systems now, but what if we can't get a signal? What if I somehow can't retrieve the information I need to follow the right directions? The hard copy is tried and true! Isn't our spiritual journey like that? Rest in Jesus as our guide, who will never fail us and will direct our wheels to the right roadway!

From Myra: While studying *Unshakable Hope* by Max Lucado, I recall 1 Peter 5:8 (ESV): "Be sober-minded; be watchful. Your adversary the devil prowls around like a roaring lion, seeking someone to devour."

My daddy taught us kids to "pay attention." He was guarding us against the dangers that come with living on the farm and working with dangerous equipment and unpredictable animals. But the warning was and is applicable to almost all aspects of life and has served me well. To guard our souls, 1 Peter is also saying, "Pay attention!"

From Doreen: God has given each of us instinct and knowledge of the difference between right and wrong. For Christians, that instinct is the Holy Spirit. Every single time I don't listen to his still, small voice, I regret it. Even if it's for something small. I've gotten much better at listening in recent years. If we are smart, we will pay attention and gain discernment to prevent harm and danger, save time, and even make our lives easier.

From Cynthia: Nearing the last portion of the journey in life, I'm in awe of those who have kept their focus on Jesus during the last leg of their journey. The golden years can be the most inspirational, and we owe God the honor and glory He deserves.

PRAYER:

Lord, as I travel down the road of life with You, help me to "trust and obey, for there is no other way to be happy in Jesus, but to trust and obey." Amen.

CHALLENGE:

Take a close look at your life. Are there paths where you need to make a U-turn and head back to the right road?

_____

_____

_____

_____

_____

_____

_____

PRIDE

 **TODAY'S PASSAGE:**

> *Pride goes before destruction, and a haughty spirit before a fall.*
>
> **Proverbs 16:18**

COMMENTARY:

From Garry: Today's proverb follows immediately after verse 17, which depicts a highway for the upright. The road traveled by the upright turns aside from evil. They avoid those wrong turns that bring destruction. In contrast, the proud person is blinded because they cannot see beyond themselves. Proverbs 8 speaks of wisdom, crying out to all who hear, offering blessing to those who listen. But the proud cannot hear because of self-centeredness and insolence. The proud and arrogant person causes strife, injuring himself as well as others.

Pride trips us up. Pride is destructive. According to Proverbs 16:18 (TPT), as stated in the Passion Translation, "Your boast becomes a prophecy of a future failure. The higher you lift yourself up in pride, the harder you'll fall in disgrace." Proverbs 18:12 (ESV) states, "Before destruction a man's heart is haughty, but humility comes before honor."

From Ward: I hope not to be counted among the proud but the humble. Pride today is seen as an attribute that shows confidence, strength, and loyalty to your actions and plans. This verse condemns the pride of those who believe themselves superior and use power to control others. Proud people in public and private settings are eventually brought down because their belief in their superiority prevents them from making righteous decisions. Yet, I have never seen or heard of a humble person experiencing shame and loss because of their actions. The humble can experience failure and collapse, but not because of their conceit. Few leaders exhibit humility. Why? Because our culture encourages lieutenants to build up and sustain the pride of the captains.

We who value humility must proclaim to the world that the humble are the true guarantors of a successful society. A good foundation for the future is built on trust, compassion, honesty, and equity, not on requiring a victory at every battle and no mercy to the vanquished. May we all choose to be humble and faithful as leaders and followers, seeing God as the source of our wisdom and not our imaginations.

From Doreen: A person's pride or arrogance can make them resistant to learning. They may be unwilling to listen to the wisdom of others, preferring instead to follow their own beliefs and way, regardless of what others say. This can lead to many problems in life, including their career, personal life, and physical health.

Honestly, I struggle with being prideful at times. Some of my accomplishments make me proud; however, I'm not an arrogant or unteachable person.

From Cynthia: Nobody wants to be considered the proud person and fall. On social media, we often encounter individuals who believe they are superior to others, particularly on contentious topics. I've never convinced anyone to change their way of thinking by trickery or pride. I'm also grateful that social media wasn't available when my words were more careless. Caring for souls is more important, and so is doing and saying the right thing.

PRAYER:

Father, may I humbly walk before You to serve others. May I be open-minded to listen and be available rather than arrogant and proud. Amen.

CHALLENGE:

Help me remember that God resists the proud but gives grace to the humble.

HUMILITY

🌳 TODAY'S PASSAGE:

> *It is better to be of a lowly spirit with the poor than to divide the spoil with the proud.*
>
> **Proverbs 16:19**

COMMENTARY:

From Garry: A lowly spirit is marked by humility and a submissive attitude before the Lord. A humble person is inoffensive and gentle. When I think about humility, I am reminded of this passage in Philippians:

> *Do nothing from selfish ambition or conceit, but in humility count others more significant than yourselves. Let each of you look not only to his own interests but also to the interests of others. Have this mind among yourselves, which is yours in Christ Jesus.*
>
> **Philippians 2:3-5 (ESV)**

This way of living is in stark contrast to the proud and overbearing who divide the plunder taken violently and wrongfully. Don't be a part of sharing the loot with them. The New International Readers Version says, "Suppose you are lowly in spirit along with those who are treated badly. That's better than sharing stolen goods with those who are proud," (Proverbs 16:19 [NIRV]).

From Ward: I am not sure our society likes humble people. The folks who are popular in the news tend to be those who promote themselves, hold predictable opinions, know whom they dislike, and quickly judge their opponents. These outlandish traits seem to me to be the opposite of humility. I wonder how humble folks can be elected leaders or serve in appointed positions. I have difficulty finding a governmental leader whom I would classify as humble. One exception is the past city councilman for our part of town, a quiet-speaking gentleman. His name rarely appeared in the news. He received little support when running for mayor. He seems to me to be a humble person who was ignored by his larger-than-life colleagues.

Jesus is the ultimate example of a humble person. He was often misunderstood when he taught and healed. Eventually, he died without defending himself, remaining nonviolent and without uttering threats. God wants us to be this type of person.

How can I learn to be humble? For myself, it is to develop the characteristics of the fruit of the spirit in Galatians 5—exhibiting love, joy, peace, patience, kindness, goodness, faithfulness, gentleness, and self-control. These are not always easy for me to do, but I try each day. May each one of us seek the way of humility and give up self-promotion so that the Lord may be glorified each day.

From Frank: I was reading in Esther today, and when the Jews defended themselves against those who were trying to destroy them, they did not take part in the plunder.

From Jim: One thing I am wrestling with is being submissive to the Lord. And that is not an easy task.

From Frank H.: Better to be poor and right with God than wealthy and corrupt.

From Cindi: Being kind to those who serve me and kindly serving others is my daily calling. The challenge comes when I encounter those who are unkind. Yes, Jesus, I am sorry for some missed opportunities when I could have shown your kind of love to someone who needed it.

From Cynthia: Every day is a gift to follow Jesus. Most days, I fall short of the mark. One day, I was tired when I saw a woman at the airport struggling to get out of her wheelchair to use the restroom. I didn't even have the energy to ask her if I could help her. Her attendant pushing the wheelchair acted like it was a burden to just wait by her wheelchair while she was gone. I was distracted by the group I was with and therefore prayed she would manage fine. Later, I wished I could go back and make a different decision.

PRAYER:

Lord, may I humbly walk with You today and find ways to serve others with the mind of Christ. Amen.

CHALLENGE:

What kind of outlook do you take as you live each day?

_____
_____
_____
_____
_____
_____
_____

TRUST IN THE LORD

 **TODAY'S PASSAGE:**

Whoever gives thought to the word will discover good, and blessed is he who trusts in the LORD.

Proverbs 16:20

COMMENTARY:

From Garry: Take the time to grasp and understand the Word. Don't rush. Be careful and pay attention to the matter at hand. Take the time to penetrate the words of God in the Scriptures. Let the Word penetrate you. When you seek to discover God's character revealed in the Scripture, you uncover nuggets of truth that give insight into how to lead a good life. Leading a good life comes from walking with God daily. As you grow in your faith, you discover God can be trusted. We can count on his wisdom, love, and power. We feel his presence and know his peace. Waiting on God is an active receptivity. He is worthy of our trust. Psalm 25 states,

To you, O LORD, I lift up my soul. O my God, in you I trust…Make me to know your ways, O LORD; teach me your paths. Lead me in your truth and teach me, for you are the God of my salvation; for you I wait all day long.

Psalm 25:1-2a, 4-5 (ESV)

From Ward: What makes you happy? I searched online and found many causes of happiness. The most mentioned cause is when a person gets what they want. Yet none of us can get what we want every day and every hour. Our culture encourages its members to pursue happiness each day. But perpetual happiness is an impossible goal. Loss, pain, and disappointment happen to everyone. In this proverb, "blessed" means happy. So, the writer tells us that if we trust in the Lord, happiness will happen.

Our world tells us we can find happiness in exciting events, connecting with others, and being enthusiastic about our lives. These goals focus on our wants and our plans. This proverb says we should focus on God, His wants, His plans, and His purpose. Yikes, it's a totally different approach to living.

How does a person trust in the Lord? Hebrews 11:6b (NIV) says, "Anyone who comes to him must believe that He exists and that He rewards those who earnestly seek him." And Psalm 34:4a (NIV) says, "I sought the LORD, and he answered me." So trusting in God means we should believe He exists and only has good intentions for us. He wants us to talk to Him, to be open and honest about our feelings and struggles.

Lastly, we should listen and watch for Him to speak and act. Having fun and accomplishing my goals is an OK way to live, but the happiness coming from those actions is fleeting. I would rather trust in the Lord each day and see what happiness comes my way. He is eternal. His love is forever. His compassion is available each day, no matter what pain or suffering we experience. Let us not focus so much on the temporary that we forget the eternal.

From Jim J.: Waiting on God is active receptivity. Well said, Garry.

From Barrett: Receiving God's Word through Bible Study, whether small and informal or large and structured, is frequently more meaningful than individual Scripture study. But there is nothing wrong with that approach in the privacy of your own mind. However, discussions of Scripture with Christians at different stages of faith deepen my understanding of God's Word. When Lewis Carroll wrote *Alice Through the Looking Glass*, he gave us this:

> "When I use a word," Humpty Dumpty said in rather a scornful tone, "it means just what I choose it to mean—neither more nor less."

> "The question is," said Alice, "whether you can make one word mean so many different things."
> "No, the question is," said Humpty Dumpty, "which is to be master—that's all."

Biblical scholars have long debated the same positions on God's Word, often with great erudition.

From Kelley: Garry, this is so insightful. Penetrate the Word and let the Word penetrate you. That genuinely gives me something to think about. Too often, we superficially read Scripture, gliding right over it without digging in and allowing it to penetrate our hearts. May the Grace and Peace of Jesus Christ be with you.

From Cynthia: With the busyness of life, it is challenging to focus on and think about Jesus daily. However, meeting with Him daily is an honor. There are even times when He gets my attention in the middle of the night (perhaps because I have not made time to be with Him during the day). I love talking with Him whenever given a chance. Jesus is a friend indeed.

From Leslie: Amen!

From Frank C.: Garry, I've been convicted of trying to "speed through" the Word and not let it penetrate. I'm slowing down and meditating more, and it is indeed rewarding.

From Cindi: For me, it is often in the quiet that The Word is heard and felt. Sometimes, I sit with it for a while (even days!) before I can see its application in my life. It's miraculous when it happens!

PRAYER:

Lord, help me today to spend time in Your word. Help me to really think about it. And help me trust Your presence and Your guidance. Amen.

CHALLENGE:

Give thought to the Word and discover the goodness of God.

_____
_____
_____
_____
_____
_____
_____

OUR SPEECH

TODAY'S PASSAGE:

The wise of heart is called discerning, and sweetness of speech increases persuasiveness. Good sense is a fountain of life to him who has it, but the instruction of fools is folly. The heart of the wise makes his speech judicious and adds persuasiveness to his lips.

Proverbs 16:21-23

COMMENTARY:

From Garry: All three proverbs were compiled because of their similar themes. The wise of heart are careful and think before they speak. Our speech can be effective when it proceeds from a heart that has wisdom.

In James 3:13 (ESV), we read, "Who is wise and understanding among you? By his good conduct let him show his works in the meekness of wisdom." Good conduct involves using discernment in what we say. Is it appropriate? Does it bless? Is it encouraging?

Ephesians 4:29 (NIV) says, "Do not let any unwholesome talk come out of your mouths, but only what is helpful for building others up according to their needs, that it may benefit those who listen." Other versions to consider are:

- "Good judgment proves that you are wise, and if you speak kindly, you can teach others," (Proverbs 16:21 [CEV]).
- "A wise, mature person is known for his understanding. The more pleasant his words, the more persuasive he is," (Proverbs 16:21 [GNT]).
- "Intelligent people think before they speak; what they say is then more persuasive," (Proverbs 16:23 [GNT]).

From Ward: What do you think when you see a fountain? I wonder where the water comes from and how much evaporates each day. Some folks will throw a coin into the fountain and hope that a wish will come true. When this proverb was written, a fountain, spring, or oasis was a source of joy. Over half of the land of Israel has a water shortage. If a group finds a permanent source of water, the community can prosper and believe there is a future for them.

The words "discerning" and "good sense" can also be translated as "understanding." When we have an understanding of a situation, it is like finding a fountain in the desert. There is great excitement. Sudden inspiration and realization can remove stress and bring peace to our minds.

The word "learning" in these verses can also be translated as "influence." When we gain insight and understanding, we can have a positive influence on others. We should never use our knowledge to manipulate, control, or embarrass others. Using our knowledge to benefit only ourselves leads to eventual emptiness. The wisdom we receive should be used to help others and make our community safe and prosperous. May all of us sit with the wise and ignore the folly of the fools.

From Cynthia: These Proverbs convict me of the times when my words were foolish. No one likes to be misunderstood, yet understanding comes from good listening. It's interesting that wise people are doing good works instead of gossiping. Hopefully, people will forgive and forget the nonsense that isn't worthy of remembering. May God lead the foolish to repentance and fill the empty hearts with His word.

From Doreen: In most tense situations, there's a better outcome if we speak in a calm voice. Praying for discernment is important. God will guide us with His Spirit if we ask. Discernment is important as well. Through prayer, I've become better at keeping my cool and not overreacting, and I've also learned to stay calm. Often, I seek God's wisdom to better serve my customers.

From Jim J.: Well said—and not always easy on a hard and/or busy day. I think I needed to think about this today. Thank you.

PRAYER:

Lord, give me a heart of wisdom. Guard my lips today. May what I speak flow from a heart that is full of Your love and grace. May all that I say bless and encourage those around me. Amen.

CHALLENGE:

Make an impact on others for good. Be a channel of God's peace in how you speak.

_____
_____
_____
_____
_____
_____
_____

GRACIOUS WORDS

 **TODAY'S PASSAGE:**

Gracious words are like a honeycomb, sweetness to the soul and health to the body.

Proverbs 16:24

COMMENTARY:

From Garry: An old Japanese proverb states, "One kind word can warm three winter months." Words are powerful. Death and life are in the power of the tongue. With our words, we can bless or we can curse. With our words, we can either do damage or offer help. Pleasant words will enliven and encourage. Gracious words are kind, thoughtful, and true. The way we communicate, through eye contact and body movements, and the tone in which we speak, can either build up or tear down. Gracious words are sweet, and they can do much good.

From Ward: Speaking and writing polite words seems out of style. I recently went online to view readers' remarks in the comment section on a specific news story. Here are words that were used to describe a current elected official:

Received a taste of his own medicine - lied - do nothing - used dirty tricks - unfit - good for nothing - self-serving - playing games - did stunts - corrupt - obnoxious - crooked - hypocrite - spineless - puppet - circus seal

I did not read any complimentary words. I doubt the comments changed any readers' opinion of this official. The written words probably soothed the writer's mind rather than the reader's. But must these descriptors be published online? Must every negative opinion be voiced? Gracious words provide health to our mind and body. What do derogatory words bring us? In the movie *Pollyanna*, the harsh words from the pastor each Sunday gave the church members sour stomachs. Our excessive use of negative words does not make the world sweet. They reinforce division, smugness, and anger.

What if, in the next week, you chose not to say any negative words aloud when talking about another person? That is, all the words describing others would be neutral or complimentary. After the week, review yourself and think if your mind is more peaceful and calmer. I believe you will know what the answer will be.

From Cindi: My Mom wasn't one to lavish compliments. When she gave me one, I relished it and can still remember her words. Maybe it is because I knew they were true and had meaning. While I do try to be more uplifting to others with my words than she was, I want others to know I am speaking in truth and with integrity. Words are powerful, and I want mine to reflect a life in Christ. It is a constant goal, and I can't do it without Jesus!

From Doreen: A compliment is always nice to hear. It blesses the giver and receiver.

From Cynthia: I'm grateful for the people who encouraged me to be the person I was meant to be. Sometimes, the truth hurts, but I knew their words were meant for good. Encouragers don't write people off because everyone is a child of God. Encouragers inspire others to finish the race. I love to read from authors who have inspired many people, such as Dallas Willard, Bob and Maria Goff, Jon Acuff, and Lisa Bevere, among others.

PRAYER:

Lord, help me be an encourager today. Help me be cheerful and kind, controlled by Your Holy Spirit. Amen.

CHALLENGE:

Let everything you say today be a blessing to others.

KNOWING RIGHT

 **TODAY'S PASSAGE:**

> *There is a way that seems right to a man, but its end is the way to death.*
> **Proverbs 16:25 and 14:12**

COMMENTARY:

From Garry: This proverb is repeated twice in the book of Proverbs. I wonder why? The term "right" refers to a shortcut to success taken by those who are impatient or possibly lazy. Alternatively, it may refer to those who want to cut corners morally to establish their own way. The Passion Translation says,

> *You can rationalize it all you want and justify the path you have chosen, but you'll find out in the end that you took the road to destruction.*
> **Proverbs 14:12 (TPT)**

 I looked back at the first book I wrote on Proverbs, *Got Wisdom Volume I,* and reviewed the comments on Proverbs 14:12. Ward wrote: "We need help to succeed. We cannot be 100 percent self-sufficient and expect to prosper." He also emphasized the importance of having other counselors, particularly those within the Body of Christ, who can support us on our life's journey. I agree with Ward.

 It is better to be safe as well as careful when choosing your path. We need each other. God has made us for community for a good reason. The phrase "way to death" implies a warning. These Proverbs understand that "death" is more than just a single physical event. Death is an entire realm in conflict with life. You can be alive yet live a way of death by straying from the wisdom God freely offers.

Proverbs 8:35-36 says:

> *For whoever finds me [wisdom] finds life and obtains favor from the LORD, but he who fails to find me injures himself; all who hate me love death.*
> **Proverbs 8:35-36 (ESV, Emphasis Added)**

From Ward: How do you know what is right? Some folks I talk to give me the answer, "I just know." Well, y'all would not want to taste any chocolate chip cookies I would make if that were the only recipe I had. There must be a standard for what is right. Consider these:

- "My Grandpa always said…."
- "The government tells us…."
- "You learn from experience…."
- "It just is…."
- "My truth may not be your truth…."

These are not terrible thoughts, but none of these are universal for every culture, location, and time.

Popular commentator Michael Medev says, "The Torah tells us what is right." As a Christian, I will expand on that and say the entire Bible tells us what is right, true, and just. And the only way to know what is in the Bible is to read it. We can never discern the totality of truth from looking inward to our soul, even though other religions and philosophies encourage this. What is right is revealed to us by God, the only Being who is totally right, true, and just. If our standard of thinking and conduct align with His, then we know what is right. Knowing God's revealed truth leads to a healthy, peaceful life. Following our own imaginations leads to death, despite what other philosophers say. May all of us reading these words take time to read the Bible and see the truths about our world and our existence.

From Frank H.: When left to our own devices, we sometimes choose a path that leads to trouble and maybe even destruction. We need you every day, Lord, for your love, wisdom, and direction.

From Cindi: Dear Lord, help me seek Your wisdom in all things, for I know I often mess things up on my own.

From Doreen: I think we're all born with a gut feeling that tells us when we're doing wrong, especially as we age. Sometimes, I feel led to do something because I know it's the right thing to do. However, my decisions are often swayed by life, negative self-talk, or external influences.

We also have habits we know deep down aren't good for us in the long run. Bad habits are hard to break. Wisdom has led me to break some long-held habits because I saw how damaging they were to others. I'm currently working on overcoming some more habits that I want to change. These are habits that may seem easy enough to break, and they're habits that most people don't think of as bad. Lord, help us make better choices.

From Jim J.: I really appreciate this one. Over the years, I have learned the value of honest feedback from friends who help me stay on track. What seemed right to me certainly may not be the right path to take.

From Cynthia: I'm embarrassed by the arguments I fueled with my pride, thinking I was correct. Students are taught that it is important to be right to succeed and advance. It takes humility to listen to another's perspective. Doing the right thing is more important than "being right."

PRAYER:

Lord, help me with my choices. May I choose wisdom. May I choose You and Your ways. May I be careful and patient. Help me listen to others who can offer their help. Amen.

CHALLENGE:

As you travel the roads of life, avoid wrong turns by walking with the right guide—Jesus.

_____
_____
_____
_____
_____
_____
_____
_____

WORK

 **TODAY'S PASSAGE:**

> *A worker's appetite works for him; his mouth urges him on.*
>
> **Proverbs 16:26**

COMMENTARY:

From Garry: At the time Proverbs was written, many Israelites worked in the fields. They knew the value of harvest and the importance of maintaining their crops. The Contemporary English Version translates Proverbs 16:26 (CEV): "The hungrier you are, the harder you work." The awareness of our physical needs and appetite for food gives us the incentive for labor. In 2 Thessalonians, we are made aware of the value of work:

> *For even when we were with you, we would give you this command: If anyone is not willing to work, let him not eat. For we hear that some among you walk in idleness, not busy at work, but busybodies. Now such persons we command and encourage in the Lord Jesus Christ to do their work quietly and to earn their own living.*
>
> **2 Thessalonians 3:10-12 (ESV)**

When the Apostle Paul wrote to the church in Ephesus, he said,

> *Let the thief no longer steal, but rather let him labor, doing honest work with his own hands, so that he may have something to share with anyone in need.*
>
> **Ephesians 4:28 (ESV)**

The writer of Ecclesiastes wrote:

> *Behold, what I have seen to be good and fitting is to eat and drink and find enjoyment in all the toil with which one toils under the sun the few days of his life that God has given him, for this is his lot.*
> **Ecclesiastes 5:18 (ESV)**

From Leslie: Good word!

From Ward: One of my grandparents would say to me, "Hard work never hurt anyone." Well, maybe this is true, but it sure makes me sore. Another one would say, "After finishing a tough task, you will be satisfied with the result." Well, maybe for some folk, but for me, I am just plain dog-gone tired. Probably because I do not feel like I am skilled at working with my hands.

Dave Ramsey has a quote: "Hunger is a great motivator." The desire to meet our physical needs, such as having food, shelter, clothing, and defense against the weather, is universal. All of us spend time and effort worrying about how to meet these needs and avoid embarrassment in front of our neighbors.

Yet Jesus tells us in Matthew 6:

> *Therefore I tell you, do not worry about your life, what you will eat or drink; or about your body, what you will wear.*
> **Matthew 6:25 (NIV)**

And later, He continues,

> *Your heavenly Father knows that you need them...and all these things will be given to you as well.*
> **Matthew 6:32b-33b (NIV)**

What, Jesus? **God** will give me what I need? I work because I must buy and earn what I need. I do not see clothes, food, and housing freely falling from the sky or arriving in a truck at my door. But I am not interpreting the Bible correctly. God requires us to *work* to meet our physical needs.

But we should *never* worry. He will use our work, along with the laws of nature, to provide for us and our family. Even in times of poverty, floods, drought, plague, and war, God can still provide for us. Our family and friends may experience death, injury, and property loss, but God still wants to provide for us. Psalm 37:25b (NIV) says, "I have never seen the righteous forsaken or their children begging bread." I believe this is true. I believe God will make provision for me.

A terrible hurricane struck the US in the past week, causing widespread devastation and loss of life. Yet, I still believe the children of God are not forsaken. God's kingdom is still being revealed in this world. We can still trust Him. Like Habakkuk says in chapter three:

> *Though...there are no grapes on the vines...no sheep in the pen and no cattle in the stalls, yet I will rejoice in the Lord." May the Lord grant all of us that type of faith.*
>
> **Habakkuk 3:17-18a (NIV)**

From Jim J.: Hungering for God is driving me onward to seek Him more.

From Cynthia: I admire those people who get things done. We learn from them. Camping is a great experience for people to learn basic daily living skills and develop a shared work ethic. The food tastes better, too, especially at Christian camps! Working so that we can give to others is a good life.

PRAYER:

Lord, may I find enjoyment in my toil and work in a way that honors You. And may I be generous with all that You have provided me. Amen.

CHALLENGE:

Work hard and be responsible in your labor.

_____
_____
_____
_____
_____
_____
_____

WORTHLESS PEOPLE

TODAY'S PASSAGE:

A worthless man plots evil, and his speech is like a scorching fire. A dishonest man spreads strife, and a whisperer separates close friends. A man of violence entices his neighbor and leads him in a way that is not good. Whoever winks his eyes plans dishonest things; he who purses his lips brings evil to pass.

Proverbs 16:27-30

COMMENTARY:

From Garry: This cluster of proverbs describes the damage caused by evil in its various expressions. The invective words spread like a scorching fire by the one who devises evil. Those words burn and destroy. A person who speaks with twisted and perverse gossip causes discord and separates friends. They are troublemakers who start fights and break up friendships. Cruel people betray their friends, leading them astray from what is good. Those who hatch crooked schemes ultimately cause trouble.

As I considered all these descriptions of a worthless person, my mind also thought of the opposite description of a peacemaker. The peacemaker is a good person, worthy of honor and respect, one who plans good, who speaks to bless, promoting life and love and harmony. I thought of a person whose words were true and trustworthy, whose words were appropriate, bringing peace that helps people work together. What a difference!

From Ward: I do not know a totally evil person. Do you? Some people do wicked acts. Why? In his writing, psychological researcher Roy Baumeister identifies four basic causes of evil.

- The desire for material benefit.
- Self-interest is threatened.

- The ends justify the means.
- Pleasure in hurting others.

The last reason is infrequent. Many people who do evil believe they are defending themselves from a worse evil. Their passion is misguided, and they are led by fear and peer pressure. They easily justify their actions as no big deal and portray their victims as deserving of what happens to them. How far some people have strayed from respecting their neighbor! Acting quickly, being insecure, and taking vengeance have precedence over discovering and establishing truth. Then, our desire to hurt as a display of strength causes more strife and division.

How do we defeat evil? Thomas Merton wrote that we must first get rid of the evil leanings within our souls: selfishness, pride, vengeance, hatred, and violence. As we do this, then we will love our neighbors as ourselves, as Jesus said, and learn to forgive one another rather than condemn others. It is not an easy task for me, but one I must follow if I want to see evil removed from this world.

From Doreen: I haven't plotted evil, but I'm guilty of gossiping. I've been much better at walking away from opportunities to gossip in recent years. Many times, the gossip we hear is incorrect or simply a story of a mistake or poor choice someone else made.

God pointed out that I'm not perfect and don't want anyone talking about me, so I don't need to talk about anyone else when they make a bad choice. Over the last decade or so, I've been working on being more positive while also trying to understand the reasons behind someone else's negativity.

For instance, I have a supervisor who has a reputation for being irritable. Some of my co-workers talk about her. I normally walk away from the conversation or point out how much stress she's under and how hard her job is. Not that it's okay at all, but she's under a lot of stress, we're shorthanded, and she doesn't seem to be a practicing believer. I pray for her and treat her with respect and kindness. Now, she's much nicer than before and not as negative as she was a few years ago.

From Barrett: A great many learned individuals in history have contemplated the message and anti-message of Proverbs, and Proverbs 16 resonates through time. Will you be a person whose words are true and trustworthy? Or a plotter of evil, a liar, and a fraud?

Hemingway said, "Today is only one day in all the days that will ever be. But what will happen in all the other days that ever come can depend on what you do today."

Sir Thomas More said, "When a man takes an oath, he's holding his own self in his own hands like water, and if he opens his fingers, then he needn't hope to find himself again."

In the clear hindsight of George Orwell after penning *1984* (he might have 'misspoke' and meant 2024), Orwell noted, "In a time of universal deceit, telling the truth becomes a revolutionary act."

When the truth can be found, it seems it is even more revolutionary today. Then again, Huxley said, "You shall know the truth, and the truth shall make you mad."

As to the man who plots evil: "Honi soit qui mal y pense." (Evil to him who thinks it.)

From Frank C.: Yes, beautifully stated.

From Jim: A challenging one, but again, one that causes me to examine myself. Thank you.

From Cindi: Jesus spoke to me in these verses. It's time to truly forgive those who have caused "heart damage." I know I can lay this at His feet and let that go. My God is my Savior and Friend.

From Cynthia: Plotting is the process of planning what's on your mind. Christians think they are immune to plotting evil, but here you have it—gossip. Gossip and hurting others with words destroy relationships. This takes planning. Drinking alcohol is part of many a plan. The love of money is part of a plan. Coveting someone's lifestyle or spouse is part of a plan.

These kinds of plans destroy churches, but we can build the Body of Christ back up by speaking the truth. We can build the Body of Christ by planning every morning in prayer. Before we leave the house and speak to another person, plan how you will listen and how you will speak. Christians can do better. Christians have the potential to make life-giving plans.

PRAYER:

Lord, as I think about all the damage done through deceitful words, may I be a positive and peaceful influence instead. Amen.

CHALLENGE:

Live a life worthy of your calling in Christ.

_____
_____
_____
_____
_____
_____
_____

A CROWN OF GLORY

 **TODAY'S PASSAGE:**

Gray hair is a crown of glory; it is gained in a righteous life.

Proverbs 16:31

COMMENTARY:

From Garry: Here is a general observation about a long life. The older person may have gray hair, a physical sign that is beautiful. Regarding Proverbs 16:31 (MSG), The Message Bible states, "Gray hair is a mark of distinction, the award for a God-loyal life." Could it be that the author is simply recognizing that a life of righteousness may lead to a longer life? The crown is the reward of right living. Good choices over time might lead to a longer life. Also, godly older adults carry dignity, and they deserve our respect.

From Ward: My family has heard me say that I get another gray hair every time I argue with my children. As a result, I have a full head of gray hair! Since it comes with age, wisdom should, too. Right living should lead to a long life. But tragedy and illness can still happen to any of us.

What is right living? It is more than following a group of rules or eating certain foods. Pastor Joseph Prince says, "Right living is the result of right believing." Being a Christian is not just changing our behavior. It is transforming our inner self to honor and worship God. Receiving good teachings about Jesus will produce faith in us, and right living will follow. When the Word of God is in us, we will produce the fruits of righteousness.

The fruit of the Spirit, as described in Galatians 5:22-23, reveals the character that develops as we pursue righteous living. Hopefully, many of our senior friends have learned this. Lord, as we age, may the knowledge of right living be manifest in us and displayed to those we meet.

From Cindi: This Proverb could save me hundreds of dollars spent at the hair salon!!!

From Frank H.: Absolutely. Long life is a gift from God.

From Cynthia: We do our children a disservice when we fail to show them that their future can be better as they age. I have always loathed the commercials and shows on TV that depicted older adults as creepy, senile, and ugly. "Help, I can't get up."

A nine-year-old girl shocked me this summer after four weeks of music camp. She couldn't stop crying and said she was going to miss me. She was going on a trip to Alaska and was sad about leaving me. I'm 67 and wasn't prepared for any student to act like this with me. She isn't from a hugging family, but she gave me a great big hug. Her parents had to help me so I wouldn't be knocked down. The encouragement we give children helps them to succeed in life—and be strong in the Spirit. Her school year is showing more improvement than her parents thought possible.

From Leslie: Yes. The only commandment in the Ten Commandments with a promise is to honor your father and mother that your days may be long. Perhaps the gray hair indicates honoring parents and a long life. Of course, some people go bald or never experience gray hair. Lol. However, in scripture, we're commanded to respect the elderly.

From Cynthia: That's beautiful, Leslie. This world is not based on love and respect. We show our love for our parents by how we treat other people. They will know we are Christians by our love. The world imposes more rules than the Ten Commandments by compartmentalizing and judging people. When we place value on the weak, we show love for all creation.

PRAYER:

Father, help me live in a way that pleases You today. Amen.

CHALLENGE:

Honor the elderly.

CONTROLLING OUR ANGER

🌳 TODAY'S PASSAGE:

Whoever is slow to anger is better than the mighty, and he who rules his spirit than he who takes a city.

Proverbs 16:32

COMMENTARY:

From Garry: Patience is better than power. Responding is better than reacting. When we carefully and thoughtfully respond, we usually get what we want. But when we react without self-control, we generally experience defeat.

My wife and I lead a small group at our church that is part of the Re-Engage ministry. It helps married couples practice biblical values in their relationships. Our lesson on communication says: "Understanding and responding respectfully to each other helps bring peace and intimacy to your relationship."

Similar proverbs are found in Proverbs 14:17 and 14:29.

- Proverbs 14:17 (MSG) states: "The hotheaded do things they'll later regret; the coldhearted get the cold shoulder."
- Proverbs 14:29 (MSG) states: "Slowness to anger makes for deep understanding; a quick-tempered person stockpiles stupidity." When we have our emotions under control and do not "fly off the handle," we communicate in a way that builds trust.

Additional verses for consideration are in Proverbs and James.

- Proverbs 18:13 (ESV) says, "If one gives an answer before he hears, it is his folly and shame."

- James 1:19-20 (ESV) says, "Know this, my beloved brothers: let every person be quick to hear, slow to speak, slow to anger; for the anger of man does not produce the righteousness of God."

From Ward: There are many reasons for being angry. Two frequent causes are feeling threatened and having a judgment about a situation or person. Anger is a natural emotion that comes to all of us, but we are not required to rage at others. This proverb states that being calm when angry is a great virtue. Yet, this is a tough act for many of us. Displaying anger with loud outbursts and aggression can bring physical discomfort and breaks in relationships. It is better not to say a harsh word than to regret saying it.

How can a person control their anger? Remain calm in a stressful time? The answer is to be prepared beforehand and to train your mind in advance. Athletes practice diligently before any game or contest. To refrain from an angry outburst, we must train our minds, too. First, we must commit ourselves to peaceful actions. When the temptation for an angry reaction comes, we should remember our commitment to be patient and kind.

When angry, we must not insult another person. Do not call others derogatory names. Speak in a calm voice. Commit not to hit the table. Do not interrupt. Be willing to lose the argument and walk away. Pause before you speak. Counting to ten before you reply is a good practice. Talk only about the subject at hand. Do not bring up old memories. Finally, try to view the circumstance from the other person's viewpoint.

These tasks are not easy to do. Also, remind yourself that self-control of your speech is an easier way to resolve a conflict. A general may take a city with great power and force, but a humble person who controls his anger will rule the city in peace.

From Frank H.: Words have the power of life and death. Therefore, don't be reactive, but choose your words with patience and wisdom.

From Cindi: As a follower of Jesus, I want to think about an appropriate response from my heart and not regret saying something harmful. I pray for forgiveness for those times I have emotionally or negatively reacted. The more I lean on Jesus and let Him be my Good Shepherd, the fewer times I find myself regretting my words.

From Frank C.: Amen!

From Leslie: A kind word turns away wrath. The Bible has a lot to say about self-control, our speech, and our responses. It is a fruit of the Spirit.

From Wright: Very good, Garry!

From Bruce: Anger is the bane of all human interactions. Anger wounds others. It is better to examine the source of our anger before lashing out or withdrawing from people we love and know.

Anger is an emotion that arises from unmet needs, unhealed hurts, and unresolved issues, often stemming from feelings of hurt. When we feel hurt, the immediate emotional reaction is anger. From anger, we move to an outward expression, like yelling, withdrawal, pouting, slander, criticism, judgment, blaming, or retaliation. Anger can also move inward to self-loathing, depression, isolation, and withdrawal from the people we know and love, damaging ourselves and others.

Self-awareness is knowing what hurts trigger our anger and setting about healing the unhealed hurts. Then we will be slow to anger and stronger than the mighty.

From Doreen: Short-tempered people make me uncomfortable. I used to have a problem with anger. God helped me improve and I rarely get angry anymore. When I feel anger welling up inside of me, I try my best to pray about it. To me, anger seems to be a reaction to not getting one's way or things not going as one thinks they should.

From Cynthia: Most of the time, anger harms those we love and ourselves. We might be afraid of what might happen, but anger breeds anxiety and negativity. We often lack self-control when we prioritize being right over doing the right thing.

PRAYER:

Lord, help me be patient and exhibit understanding today. May I exercise self-control as I listen to those around me. Amen.

CHALLENGE:

Let God control all your responses as you seek to listen first.

ROLLING THE DICE

 **TODAY'S PASSAGE:**

The lot is cast into the lap, but its every decision is from the LORD.

Proverbs 16:33

COMMENTARY:

From Garry: Sometimes, the Israelites would find themselves unsure about a matter they were dealing with. For example, choosing officers—civil or ecclesiastical, dividing inheritances, or determining doubtful cases. The leaders would cast lots. These may have been colored stones that had a distinguishing mark. They were placed in a vessel or in the fold of a garment and drawn out. The people would "cast lots," intending to seek divine direction, looking to God to guide the process, and trusting the outcome.

An example of casting lots is in Joshua 7. Through this procedure, it was revealed to Joshua which tribe and which individual was responsible for the sin that caused Israel to be defeated in an earlier battle. The casting of lots determined who was responsible. The guilty party was then confronted about his theft.

From Ward: Making difficult decisions is tough for me. I delay and hope someone else will decide, or the circumstances will change, and I do not have to decide. In the Old Testament, God approved of using lots to make decisions. I do not think many of us do this today. What are some ways to help me make up my mind?

- Set a clear objective.
- Know what your goal is.
- Figure out what the alternatives are.
- Get the input of others who are competent and have knowledge about the concern.

You are not required to make an important decision alone. Take the time to think and set a deadline.

After you have decided, trust the Lord will guide you in the implementation. Believe if the decision needs an adjustment or change, God will clearly show you. The map app on your phone is not always correct. U-turns are acceptable in God's kingdom. I am not so proud that I cannot let God help me change direction when it is needed. Also, I realize when a difficult choice appears, God may take some time to give help. May all of us trust in the goodness of the Lord each day.

From Cindi: For me, a part of faith is not having to know the exact outcome. It is resting in the truth that God is good, and God is with me. It is waiting on the Lord for understanding and perhaps "course correction!"

From Leslie: God is absolutely sovereign! That's what came to mind as I read this verse.

From Doreen: This works (casting lots). We have used this method many times when we're unsure of what God wants us to do.

PRAYER:

Lord, we can trust You to guide us, even in those situations that are unclear. Help us trust You and know that, ultimately, You are in control. Amen.

CHALLENGE:

Believe that God is sovereign.

_____
_____
_____

PEACE AND QUIET

 **TODAY'S PASSAGE:**

Better is a dry morsel with quiet than a house full of feasting with strife.

Proverbs 17:1

COMMENTARY:

From Garry: Just a stale piece of bread, along with peace and quiet in the home, is better than a house that has lots of sumptuous feasting accompanied by strife. A word that stands out to me from today's passage is "better." The quality of family relationships is better than the quantity of food on the table.

The Message Bible says, "A meal of bread and water in contented peace is better than a banquet spiced with quarrels," (Proverbs 17:1 [MSG]). This proverb describes a setting where there can be carefree ease because of the sense of peace and security. Just a simple meal in a serene setting is better than a big feast where there is envy and strife.

The Good News Translation puts it like this: "Better to eat a dry crust of bread with peace of mind than have a banquet in a house full of trouble," (Proverbs 17:1 [GNT]).

From Ward: When I was a teen, my older brother and our father would argue while we were eating dinner. At this time, the major public topic of conversation was the war in Vietnam. I cannot remember what issues my brother and my father would disagree about, but there sure was a lot of noise and loud words. This did not make for a peaceful dinner for my mother and me. One time, the discussion became so heated that I went into the bathroom and threw up my dinner. I was distraught over the tension in our house.

This is not how dinner time should be for a family. A house full of feasting with strife is a distressing situation that can bring emotional scars to any family member. F. Scott Fitzgerald wrote:

> *Family quarrels are bitter things. They do not go according to any rules. They are not like aches or wounds, they are more like splits in the skin that will not heal, because there is not enough material.*

What can a family do? The goal should be forgiveness. We should not allow the memories of past arguments to cause permanent separation in family relationships. As we practice forgiveness and kindness, emotional healing can occur. May all of us not be so bound to our opinions that we cannot eat in peace with our family.

From Barrett: One as smart as Sherlock Holmes once similarly noted (likely unaware of Proverbs 17): "A dog reflects the family life." Whoever saw a frisky dog in a gloomy family, or a sad dog in a happy one? Snarling people have snarling dogs." Mean, snarling dogs are not the product of harmonious households.

Even Lincoln famously noted, "I care not for a man's religion whose dog and cat are not the better for it." Better a quiet home, whose humans and pets enjoy the dry morsel of the happy house.

From Cindi: A warm, welcoming table with friends and family gathered and sharing good things—both edible and from the heart—brings peace and joy! I've learned I don't have to fret over the preparations! It's the gathering in love that's most important!

From Doreen: In my opinion, strife causes anxiety. It does for me.

From Cynthia: People with the gift of hospitality are very admirable. Joy and love fill the homes that are graced with love and respect. The welcome mat is always out when one has this gift.

PRAYER:

Lord, bless our home. Guide the way we relate to one another. May our family be at peace. Amen.

CHALLENGE:

Think about the atmosphere of your home. What can you do to help create a sense of peace?

_____
_____
_____
_____
_____
_____
_____

SERVING FAITHFULLY

🌳 TODAY'S PASSAGE:

> *A servant who deals wisely will rule over a son who acts shamefully and will share the inheritance as one of the brothers.*
>
> Proverbs 17:2

COMMENTARY:

From Garry: In consulting commentaries and websites related to this proverb, I came across the Calvary Chapel of Jonesboro's website, *A Proverb a Day*. (http://calvarychapeljonesboro.org/proverb-a-day.html). Quoting directly, it says:

> The servant who acts wisely and respectfully will eventually rule over the shameful son. A truly wise father will not give all to his son if his son is a fool. It is better to transfer wealth and influence on a godly and wise servant—than to a son who will only waste that wealth and destroy any future for a family business. That faithful servant often will share in the inheritance among all the other brothers—not because of a blood relationship—but due to a lifetime of service to the master...when we manifest a servant's heart to our employer—showing both wisdom and respect in the workplace—honor will come our way. Cultivate a servant's heart in all that you do. In this proverb, the man with the true servant's heart is honored. You will never regret developing and manifesting a servant's heart toward others. Even if you are not honored on earth or at your job, God Himself will honor you for living this way. Embrace the role of servant whenever you can.

From Ward: My grandmother took great pleasure in thinking about her ancestors. She would fondly tell my brother and me stories of how the family moved from Germany to southern Illinois and then to St. Louis, where they became established and transitioned to living in a new country. Since I had never met these people, I couldn't easily understand the details of their stories. However, her family's past and her memories were important to her.

Our family's past can bring great memories, but our actions today are the basic concerns of living in our community. God focuses his attention on our present state and our future. He knows we are more than our past experiences. Our past may influence us, but it should never enslave us. God wants to use our talents for good today so that we can grow as disciples of Jesus tomorrow. As we allow God to regenerate us, we can let go of past mistakes and walk into a new future. Anyone can receive the inheritance of God, which is life in His kingdom, if we become followers of Jesus. Our family name is not important to being God's child. Our love for God, our true Father, is.

From Barrett: Angels serve others in heaven and on earth with a servant's heart. On earth, mortals with serving hearts serve others through a range of simple acts of kindness. They may hold a door for someone, help to carry a burden, provide full-time caregiving, or provide professional care and support to clients. Those who are served become masters of the servant's heart in kindness. Perhaps lesser to greater angels exist, hence Archangels. Some mortals elect to serve others here on earth; they deserve the status of earthly angels, angels of mercy. It is all about kindness. Albert Schweitzer said, "As the sun makes ice melt, kindness causes misunderstanding, mistrust, and hostility to evaporate."

From Cindi: To serve out of love without expecting any reward is living in freedom! No disappointment, no anger, no anxiety, and no scheming required! Where the Spirit of the Lord is, there is freedom!

From Doreen: This is true. I have seen it happen. People who work hard and show that they're trustworthy, respectful, and responsible tend to have better experiences in their jobs and lives overall.

From Cynthia: We are commanded to love one another. A servant's heart is the blueprint to love. Going on a Walk to Emmaus was an overwhelming weekend surrounded by servants' hearts.

PRAYER:

Lord, give me a faithful servant's heart in all I do. Amen.

CHALLENGE:

True wisdom is found in serving others faithfully.

_____
_____
_____
_____
_____
_____
_____

THE CRUCIBLE REFINES US

 **TODAY'S PASSAGE:**

The crucible is for silver, and the furnace is for gold, and the LORD tests hearts.
Proverbs 17:3

COMMENTARY:

From Garry: When we are in a trial, and our situation is difficult, that is the time to recognize that the Lord is working for our benefit. As we become increasingly aware of the areas in our lives that are dross and need attention, we can trust that God is at work. God knows our hearts. The Holy Spirit reveals what is in our hearts and helps us know ourselves better so we can partner with God to grow.

The Passion Translation states, "In the same way that gold and silver are refined by fire, the Lord purifies your heart by the tests and trials of life," (Proverbs 17:3 [TPT]). In the notes for the New English Translation, it is pointed out that the "crucible" is the place or instrument of refining. Remember that it is the Lord who tests the hearts. Tests, in all their forms, add value to those undergoing them. When this testing occurs, evil and folly will be removed.

From Ward: I do not like to suffer. I dislike being uncomfortable. When my house is a little too cold or a little too hot, I feel like I am being denied a pleasant life. God did not promise me or anyone who has ever lived a trouble-free life.

The first two people who lived in God's garden endured no pain, no sweat, no loss, no injury, no unhappiness, and no tough work. The first couple only had to obey one commandment to maintain this life. Not ten, just one. And they could not do that. So, God told them they must leave the stress-free garden and go into a world containing suffering, lack of fulfillment, frustration, and backbreaking work.

Over many centuries, humans have invented and produced products and structures that help us overcome many tragedies of living. Yet even with all the comforts we possess now, we cannot prevent all death, illness, accidents, and weather-related destruction. We are stuck in a world and time that is far from what the original garden had. Our pain is not a punishment for what we have thought or done but a consequence of not being fully connected to our Father God and His purposes.

So, what is a good response? Ask God to forgive our wrongdoings, ask for His guidance, and commit to acting godly in every situation. Stop blaming God for any less-than-perfect circumstance we are in. God's desire is to comfort us in the time of trouble, not to make the situation worse. God allows suffering so we can seek comfort from Him, and then He allows us to comfort others. If we comfort others who are suffering, we can help redeem the pain that has come.

Let us not yield to anger and resentment when we suffer pain, but instead allow ourselves to develop a closer relationship with God.

From Kyle: The following commentary sheds light on today's passage, taken from the Calvary Chapel of Jonesboro's website, titled "Proverb A Day." (https://www.calvarychapeljonesboro.org/proverb-a-day/hearts-of-silver-and-gold-Proverbs 17:3)

> [Silver is purified by being placed] into a crucible or refining pot and heated to very high temperatures so that the dross can be scraped off the top. What is left is highly purified silver. Gold is similar in that the higher the purity, the higher the value. Thus, gold is put into a furnace to accomplish the same process. What this proverb says is that what the pot is to the silver, and the furnace is to gold, God is to the hearts of men.
>
> ...We find that process of trial and testing [not much fun]. It is hard—and often it is stressful. [Testing and trial] is difficult to encounter—and many times it reveals rather embarrassing sins in our lives. Yet as the dross is lifted off our hearts in this process—there comes out something that God can mightily use.

Am I volunteering for trials and testing?...No, but I know that if I want to draw nearer to the Lord and be further conformed into the image of His beloved Son, they are coming...In this process, [I have a comforting reminder that] the Lord does not have it out for me. To the contrary, this is done out of His utmost love and desire for me to know Him better and reflect the heart of His son. Remember this next time you find yourself in the refining pot. He loves you through it all—and more than anything else, all this is working to show forth the glorious perfections of His Son within you.

From Doreen: This verse has taught me to pray for God to help me learn what he wants me to do when I'm going through a tough time.

From Cynthia: We learn from our trials, and others get to witness the show. When trials are completed, or if the worst is over, the ministry involved is easier to see. A trial can be a ministry, though difficult to understand, especially when everyone can see how imperfect you are.

PRAYER:

Lord, thank You for knowing me and for changing me. Thank You for revealing what is deep inside of me and for exposing those areas of sin in my life that need to change. May I be more like You. Amen.

CHALLENGE:

Realize the truth from Hebrews:

> *[God] disciplines us for our good, that we may share his holiness. For the moment, all discipline seems painful rather than pleasant, but later it yields the peaceful fruit of righteousness to those who have been trained by it.*
> **Hebrews 12:10b-11 (ESV, Emphasis Added)**

EVIL FEEDS ON EVIL

 **TODAY'S PASSAGE:**

An evildoer listens to wicked lips, and a liar gives ear to a mischievous tongue.
Proverbs 17:4

COMMENTARY:

From Garry: It is the nature of an evildoer to eagerly listen to evil talk. Wicked, self-serving people find destructive speech appealing. The Contemporary English Version says, "Troublemakers listen to troublemakers, and liars listen to liars," (Proverbs 17:4 [CEV]). Evil feeds on evil. Liars listen to lies.

The Message Bible says, "Evil people relish malicious conversation; the ears of liars itch for dirty gossip," (Proverbs 17:4 [MSG]). This is an observation about those who cause trouble and turmoil throughout their lives. Watch out for those who cause trouble.

From Ward: With whom do you hang out? Who are your friends and acquaintances? Almost all the people we frequently encounter and spend time with share a similar household income, moral and political views, educational background, and often a similar ethnicity and skin color. Frank Sonnenberg has written, "You are only as good at the company you keep." This seems true. People who are up to no good often spend time with others who behave similarly. If you want to have good moral character, then you should spend time with people who display good moral character.

Paul writes in 1 Corinthians 15:33 (NIV), "Bad company corrupts good character." Our closest relationships affect our behavior and thinking. Few people live totally isolated from others. And to do so is not healthy for our mental state. I encourage you this week to thank God for the people He has placed in your life who have had a positive and upright influence on you. If possible, take a moment to tell them, "Thank you."

From Leslie: I love your prayer. Yes, Lord, give me a discerning spirit. Help me know Your truth so that I can recognize that which is not.

From Jim J.: Itchy ears continue to manifest as part of human sinful nature today in the media and other ways.

From Barrett: American novelist Patricia Cornwell wrote: "If we can't recognize evil, then we can't say for sure it's not in our midst," (from *Chaos*). The corollary to that is if we refuse to recognize evil exists, then we invite it into our midst, where Satan will dominate our lives. A popular agenda today focuses on the evils of so-called 'injustice'—sometimes real, most often imaginary. However, noted poet Jack Gilbert observed the danger in that "To make injustice the only measure for our attention is to praise the Devil."

From Doreen: Evil and/or angry people look for reasons to hate and be angry, or even talk about it with others. If you look for good, you can find it. Many TV shows and news outlets focus on evil and negativity.

From Cynthia: God's truth is the measurement to resist liars and evildoers. The world is persuasive, and I hope that truth always reaches me and those I love.

PRAYER:

Lord, may I speak truth, and be aware of those who twist it. Amen.

CHALLENGE:

You can trust those who tell the truth. Watch out for those who love to deceive.

_____

_____

DO NOT MOCK THE POOR

TODAY'S PASSAGE:

Whoever mocks the poor insults his Maker; he who is glad at calamity will not go unpunished.

Proverbs 17:5

COMMENTARY:

From Garry: Do not rejoice over the disaster that comes to the disadvantaged and the poor. Do not make fun of anyone's misfortune. If you do, you are insulting God, their creator. The Hebrew word *insult* means to taunt. It shows contempt. When you reproach God by blaming his providential control of the world and ignore the complications of poverty, you reveal a callous attitude towards those in need. Their poverty may not be a result of personal failure.

This proverb implies God has a special concern for the poor. Proverbs 14:31 (ESV) says, "Whoever oppresses a poor man insults his Maker, but he who is generous to the needy honors him." You honor God when you treat the poor with dignity and are generous to those in need. You dishonor God when you look down on the poor or think you are better than them.

From Ward: My mother told me when I was a teen that the poor in America are invisible. In many nations of the world, the poor are easily seen. They beg on the street, have no permanent housing, lack sufficient food for each day, are dressed in rags, and have no medical care.

In the United States, numerous government agencies and private organizations are available to assist those in need. So, the poor will have clothes, food to eat, and often a part-time job. The poor often suffer from underemployment, which is having a job but not earning enough money to meet their monthly needs. A comment I have heard is that the poor should work harder if they wish to escape poverty. This statement implies that the poor in our nation are responsible for their situation and, therefore, to blame for their lack of success.

God does not want us to judge the less fortunate. Many poor people know the Lord. So, they are our brothers and sisters in Christ, not aliens from another planet. Almost everyone reading this message has received great benefits and gifts from God that make their life comfortable. We do not enjoy the wealth we have solely because of our own efforts.

Many poor people, on the other hand, have not received these gifts because of life events. Our duty is to help our brothers and sisters who are trapped in poverty by assisting them with permanent change in their lives. Saying degrading comments and turning a blind eye to them does not constitute "loving one another." If you give a dollar or a food snack to a person in need at a street intersection, please do so with a smile and grace. If the stoplight is long enough, ask the person their name and tell them you will pray for them. Offering dignity to the less fortunate is a tangible way to show love.

From John: I was very fortunate to have been married to a lady for just over 50 years. I learned from her life that our many blessings from the Lord necessitate helping others. She taught me how to look for those who needed help, and because of that, our list of those we helped was long. She changed me because she believed in helping others with the blessings our Lord gave freely to us.

From Doreen: This verse can apply to life, not just to the poor. My struggle is not being able to help every person I meet who is in need. I know God blesses me when I help. If I give money, I usually have Satan whispering in my ear, telling me they will spend it on things they don't need. I pray for the money to bless them and let God deal with how they spend it.

I know that there are organizations that have grown large under the guise of "helping the needy." That's for God to tend to, though. Not me. I need to pray for God to give me the strength to help more without harboring judgment in my heart, especially towards someone I often see at my workplace.

From Cynthia: The poor allow us to be blessed when they receive our kindness or help. My generation was affluent in the 70s. Some continued to thrive, and most had a great education. Since 2020, it has become easier to notice more people who are poor in spirit or poor in assets. Many retirees must return to work to make ends meet. Our government has not properly addressed inflation.

I wonder if my grandchildren will ever know God's truth is the measurement to resist liars and evildoers. The world is persuasive and convinces some not to follow God. I hope Truth will always reach me and those I love. I hope my loved ones will be able to purchase a home 20 years from now. The only solution to helping the poor is to extend a helping hand, with God's grace, to those individuals the Holy Spirit reveals to us.

PRAYER:

Lord, may I treat all people with the respect and dignity they deserve because they are made in Your image, regardless of their material status. Amen.

CHALLENGE:

> *Whoever despises his neighbor is a sinner, but blessed is he who is generous to the poor.*
>
> **Proverbs 14:21 (ESV)**

_____
_____
_____
_____
_____

THE BEAUTY OF FAMILY

TODAY'S PASSAGE:

Grandchildren are the crown of the aged, and the glory of children is their fathers.

Proverbs 17:6

COMMENTARY:

From Garry: The family is God's gift. It was the first institution established by God, serving as the foundation for the well-being of society. The family is the transmitter of the values of the parents. Grandparents are part of that family unit. What makes the grandparents proud is the good character that they see in their grandchildren. They are like a crown that brings joy and honor to the family unit. In Biblical culture, both lineage and legacy are highly valued. A godly family that exhibits unity and love is a building block of an orderly society.

Author Jim Burns wrote a book entitled *The Ten Building Blocks for a Happy Family*. Here are the ten building blocks:

- The power of being there for your children is a sign of caring and connectedness.
- In parenting, affirmation, warmth, and encouragement create a secure home.
- A happy family grows from healthy morals and values.
- Clearly expressed expectations and consistent follow-through of guidance and discipline produce responsible kids.
- A happy family eliminates stress by giving time, rest, and balance to their schedule.
- Positive communication is the language of love.
- Play is necessary because it enhances togetherness and communication.
- Loving your spouse brings hope and security to the children.

- Healthy stewardship and sound financial decisions produce positive family priorities.
- Energize your family's spiritual growth and leave a spiritual legacy for your children.

From Ward: In the Bible, there are three ways of organizing people: the government, the body of believers, and the family. For the original readers of the scriptures, the family was the most important part of daily existence. The births of children and grandchildren were very exciting events, as the family had the opportunity to grow and exist in the future. Children were assets, bringing happiness and value to the entire extended family. This thought was prominent throughout the world until the end of World War I.

During and after that time, children were viewed as costing a family money and taking fun from a couple. Even today, our media highlights the cost of raising even just one child and the burdens a mother and father have that a childless couple does not. So, children are seen as taking value from a family, not adding to it.

As a result, in Western culture, childbirth rates are low. Nations that still value children continue to have population growth. In the past, the lack of having children meant traditions, wisdom, and morals would not be passed on. And that new arrivals to the community would establish new traditions and morals.

Today, in the United States, many people worry that this is happening here. We must not worry. We must not be afraid. God is still the God of the universe. Rather than lamenting any loss of past moral standards, we should take the challenge to reaffirm what God wants for this world. Let us politely and positively proclaim God's truth about families. At the same time, let us not judge and belittle those whom we assume do not accept the same morals and ethics that we might have.

From Leslie: This really resonates as we just had our first grandchild. What a blessing from God.

From Jim: Wonderful comments. The ten building blocks I found to be helpful tools for contemplating my own children and grandchildren during this time we live in. As a grandfather, I have been blessed to see how my presence in their lives has a part in shaping their own spiritual life. Thank you for this one—such thoughts are needed in our world today.

From Frank C.: Amen! Beautiful reflection.

From Cindi: Nothing compares to a close-knit, loving family! Watching children grow up and become caring, happy adults has been a great joy. Now, watching their children grow and loving them has multiplied the joy by a million! Lord, help us uplift families and support them!

From Doreen: I'm not a grandparent yet, but I have seen how happy my parents and other family members were around their grandchildren. I know it will be exciting when my kids marry and have kids of their own. We're enjoying seeing how much our sons enjoy hanging out with us when we're able to get together.

PRAYER:

Lord, as grandparents, we are so thankful for our grandchildren. They are our crown. Bless them and bless their parents, who mold and shape them as they grow. Amen.

CHALLENGE:

Consider the power of your family and thank God for it.

_____
_____
_____
_____

TRUTH CAN BE TRUSTED

 **TODAY'S PASSAGE:**

Fine speech is not becoming to a fool; still less is false speech to a prince.
                                                            Proverbs 17:7

COMMENTARY:

From Garry: When I researched this proverb, I discovered that the original Hebrew term describing the speech could mean either "arrogant" or "excellent." It also has the connotation of "excessive." Here are some other versions of today's passage:

- "Too much talking isn't right for a fool; even less so false speech for an honorable person," (Proverbs 17:7 [CEB]).
- "It is not proper for a leader to lie and deceive, and don't expect excellent words to be spoken by a fool," (Proverbs 17:7 [TPT]).
- "Respected people do not tell lies, and fools have nothing worthwhile to say," (Proverbs 17:7 [GNT]).

The current environment that we live in today is full of lies and blaming one another. Unfortunately, the last presidential election was full of targeting the opposing candidate. Honorable people, especially leaders, should be careful not to be excessive in their words. They should also be truthful in their speech.

From Ward: I wish I had an electronic device that I could attach to my computer so that when I was online, I could quickly determine fact from fiction and truth from lie. Alas, no such instrument exists. Opinion polls now seem to be the standard for correctness.

For centuries, fine speech was recognized as someone speaking with eloquence and certainty, using multi-syllable words and a loud voice, and citing facts the audience had already accepted. But fine speech does not equal truth and accuracy. The only way to discern truth today is to have been acquainted with it yesterday. As we spend time reading the Bible, we will become acquainted with the truth. Then, we can apply what we have learned to today's situation. Murder is always wrong. Theft is always wrong. Giving false testimony is always wrong. We cannot let articulate speakers convince us otherwise.

Every century has orators who make the community comfortable in its lifestyle. Yet God wants us to bring healing to the sick, sustenance to the poor, and justice to the crushed. This requires us to seek righteous change and moral improvement in our society. And not to be deceived by anyone who says all is well or that change is hopeless. Let us remember our goal:

> *For the earth will be filled with the knowledge of the glory of the LORD as the waters cover the sea.*
>
> **Habakkuk 2:14 (ESV)**

From Leslie: This is a good word. I was thinking of politicians as well—they should read the Proverbs.

From Cindi: Speaking the truth is good, but constantly flaunting our opinions is just as bad as lying! Lord, help me use wisdom and compassion in my responses.

From Jim: Excellent and timely. Thank you, Garry.

From Doreen: Keep your speech simple, which is what I've heard is best. A fool is usually only interested in what they have to say. And if you lie, you must try to remember what you said—no matter who the person is with whom you are talking.

From Cynthia: A fool thinks he's right. A wise person does the right thing and listens. God is the master of unlimited thinking, so we can be disciplined to live an abundant life.

PRAYER:

Lord, help me be respectful and honorable in my speech. May I always speak the truth. Amen.

CHALLENGE:

A wise person speaks the truth and can be trusted. Fools deceive and manipulate.

_____
_____
_____
_____
_____
_____
_____

THE BRIBE

 **TODAY'S PASSAGE:**

A bribe is like a magic stone in the eyes of the one who gives it; wherever he turns he prospers.

Proverbs 17:8

COMMENTARY:

From Garry: At first glance, this proverb seems to be an observation that a bribe has power. As I reflected on it, I thought of the phrase "money talks."

Proverbs 17:8 (CJB) from The Complete Jewish Bible says, "A bribe works like a charm, in the view of him who gives it—wherever it turns, it succeeds." The New Century Version of Proverbs 17:8 (NCV) says it this way: "Some people think they can pay others to do anything they ask. They think it will work every time."

Could it be that the author is simply making the point that those who use bribery meet with widespread success? That does not mean they are endorsing bribery. The Tyndale Old Testament Commentary on Proverbs pointed out that this perspective describes the briber's confidence in the versatile usefulness of his tool. But a proverb taken in isolation is not enough. It is good to keep in mind verses 15 and 23 of this same chapter:

- "He who justifies the wicked and he who condemns the righteous are both alike an abomination to the LORD," (Proverbs 17:15 [ESV]).
- "The wicked accepts a bribe in secret to pervert the ways of justice," (Proverbs 17:23 [ESV]).

A bribe might have power to influence, but that does not make it right.

From Ward: Giving a bribe says possessions are more important than honesty, and wealth is more important than truth. It maintains that winning is more important than following the rules, and my happiness is the only goal. Bribery cooperates with secrecy, lying, and deceit. Too many aspects of our culture use bribery to accomplish tasks rather than an open display of our actions. Wealth should not become so important that fair competition and open discussion are dismissed. Bribery uses darkness to control us. When our actions are in the light, sin loses its power over us.

We must be clear and honest in our personal relationships, too. True friendship does not involve bribery or extortion. Jesus never used bribery or extortion to defeat evil and sin. He was open about his goals, and His actions could be seen by His followers. Jesus said in Luke:

> *Nothing is covered up that will not be revealed or hidden that will not be known.*
>
> **Luke 12:2 (ESV)**

When all my secrets are revealed, I do not want to be embarrassed. Let's commit to being gentle, kind, and upright in all our actions and speech so God's kingdom may receive glory and not our bank account.

From Barrett: Sadly, there are a great many people—way too many—who believe that justice perverts bribery.

From Cindi: Lord, protect us from all types of manipulation! Give us wisdom and discernment.

From Doreen: In my nutrition classes, bribery is one subject discussed. They taught how bribery from food lobbyists allows ingredients to be added to our country's food that are not permitted in other countries. Sadly, today bribery helps people gain a lot of friends, business, and power.

From Cynthia: As parents, we resort to bribery or manipulation to get things done quickly and efficiently. It seems right at the time, and later, we might be called out on it. We learn this behavior at a young age.

PRAYER:

Father, may I be honest in all my dealings and reflect Your character in all my business. Amen.

CHALLENGE:

Never pervert justice with bribery.

TRUE FRIENDSHIP

 **TODAY'S PASSAGE:**

> *Whoever covers an offense seeks love, but he who repeats a matter separates close friends.*
>
> **Proverbs 17:9**

COMMENTARY:

From Garry: True friendship is a treasure. How do we guard it? A good friend loves by overlooking faults and forgiving the mistakes their friend makes. How we respond to the faults of others reveals whether or not we love them. If we keep bringing up the matter, we probably have not truly overlooked it. Negatively focusing on the past destroys friendships. "Hatred stirs up strife, but love covers all offenses," (Proverbs 10:12 [ESV]).

Other translations of today's passage provide a more complete understanding:

- "Love overlooks the mistakes of others, but dwelling on the failures of others devastates friendships," (Proverbs 17:9 [TPT]).
- "You will keep your friends if you forgive them, but you will lose your friends if you keep talking about what they did wrong," (Proverbs 17:9 [CEV]).

My good friend, G. Wright Doyle, wrote a book entitled *Worship and Wisdom*. He observed that in our dealings with others, we shall often be hurt.

> *If we take offense at every perceived insult or injury, we shall never have peace. There is a better way: to "cover" the other's transgression with our love. Hide*

> *it from our own eyes. Expel it from our memory. Refuse to dwell on it in our minds. This will all be easier if we refrain from telling anyone else.*
>
> G. Wright Doyle

From Ward: Let me make a confession to you—if you promise not to tell anyone else. I talk about other people's situations too much. I fall into the trap of sharing prayer concerns with too much detail and gossip. In 2 Corinthians 12:20, Paul puts gossip in the same category as anger, hostility, and disorder. Gossip seems harmless to most of us, being in the same class as "catching up on the latest news."

What makes gossip a sin and an action we should stay away from? Gossip focuses on the past. Gossip is mostly negative and demeaning. When we gossip about others, we focus on their mistakes and cast them as less valuable than ourselves. Gossip does not allow for forgiveness or the ability to change.

God is not this way. God knows where we have come from, but focuses on what we can become. God focuses little on an individual's past but challenges us to move into godliness in the future. Jesus came to the world to set the prisoner free, not allowing us to be chained to our past. God knows who we can become and gives us opportunities to make that happen. Biblical words describing what our conversation should be like include "encourage," "comfort," and "build up." Let these words guide our speech as we stop spreading negative comments about those we know.

From Doreen: It's better to forgive than to gossip. A few years ago, God helped me realize I don't want people talking about me, so I don't need to talk about others. When the devil tries to get me to talk about people or get angry with them, I pray for God to help me forgive them. I also rebuke the bad thoughts put in my head by the devil. I live a more peaceful life now.

From Myra: Truer words have never been spoken. Hardly easy, but God aims to protect us and give us peace that comes with forgiveness. My father was not an educated man, but was quite wise. He told us, his children, the same thing your friend G. Wright Doyle observed: "In your dealings with others, you shall often be hurt."

We didn't really understand, but experience proved Dad right. Despite that, I have found that having friendships is worth the risk of being hurt and gives us an opportunity to give and receive forgiveness.

From Cindi: Ruminating over past hurts and wrongs will never lead to peace. It may lead to bitterness and loneliness, though!

From Leslie:

> *Above all, keep loving one another earnestly since love covers a multitude of sins.*
>
> **1 Peter 4:8 (ESV)**

From Frank: This proverb really spoke to me. Thank you.

PRAYER:

Lord, help me be a true friend to those I love by overlooking their faults and letting them go. Amen.

CHALLENGE:

Be strong in the grace that is in Christ Jesus.

RECEPTIVE OR RESISTANT?

 **TODAY'S PASSAGE:**

> *A rebuke goes deeper into a man of understanding than a hundred blows into a fool.*
>
> **Proverbs 17:10**

COMMENTARY:

From Garry: Be open to learn and grow. There is value in being receptive to constructive criticism. Don't be like a fool who never learns and is resistant to accepting correction. The Contemporary English Version says, "A sensible person accepts correction, but you can't beat sense into a fool," (Proverbs 17:10 [CEV]).

My friend, G. Wright Doyle, points out that being receptive to criticism can be a gift from God. God knows what we need to hear. As we listen to others' criticism, let us open our minds to what God may be saying to us through their words. Even if we think the rebuke is inaccurate, we can still benefit from it. It adds to our knowledge of the other person and how we relate to him.

Another way we can reflect on this verse is to be aware of how a fool is understood in Proverbs. Fifty times in Proverbs, the term *fool* is used to describe a person who chooses to be dull and obstinate. This kind of fool has no insight into wisdom but imagines it is something that can be simply handed over to him. He cannot imagine himself mistaken. It is a spiritual issue because he likes his folly and keeps returning to it.

Another word for *fool* in Proverbs is used 19 times, and it refers to someone who is stubborn and unrestrained. He is impatient with all advice and has a flippant attitude toward sin.

A third term for *fool* in Proverbs is used three times and is like the previous terms, but it stresses being ill-mannered or rude. This fool's mind is closed to God and reason.

From Ward: This proverb employs the word *rebuke*, which refers to a harsh correction spoken to someone. I do not like to hear anyone being rebuked. The writer is not encouraging the reader to admonish his friends. Nor does he want us to hit an independent-minded person one hundred times. This proverb is one of exaggeration and contrast. This means we do not do the actions in the passage. The purpose of the words is to reveal a truth: the truth being that a person of understanding should be teachable. Garry states this eloquently in his comment.

Teaching through contrast is often used by Biblical writers. Many famous characters in Biblical stories do not act righteously. The authors of these stories want the reader to see that we should avoid ungodly acts because of the consequences that happen in the story. A professor I had in college once told our class, "You can learn as much from a bad book as you can from a good book, if you know why the bad book is bad." The same is true with stories, songs, and proverbs of contrast. Let us not be so certain that we possess complete knowledge of our beliefs that we cannot remain open to receiving new lessons from God. And let us not be so independent-minded that others think they must strike a blow to get us to understand a new thought.

From Frank C.: When I was active in a disciple-making ministry, we said we were looking for FAT guys: Faithful, Available, Teachable. Being teachable is so important.

From Frank H.: A wise person accepts criticism, learns from it, and applies it to their life. However, it does not penetrate the heart of a fool; it is shed like water off a duck.

From John: For most of us, especially me, many years ago, it was hard to accept criticism concerning our lives or the way we live. I must agree that criticism for the sake of criticism is still hard for me to accept. But constructive criticism is totally different. There were times when I felt like an expert on a subject. However, I later learned my expertise on that topic was limited, not the definitive word on the subject.

Over the years, I have learned that when a group of people gets together to discuss a certain subject, everyone has valid input. Through listening, I can learn a tremendous amount by respecting and learning from others' perspectives.

Constructive criticism is something I always try to give. My hope is to help the position or situation and not just give criticism for the sake of criticism.

From Cindi: As a musician, I have had to listen to coaching and criticism. This has allowed me to grow, improve, and be the best I can be. I am working on accepting more personal criticisms without being mortified! Pride and perfectionism can keep me from being open to criticism. This proverb is rich!

From Cindy: I believe that being teachable is one of the most important things you can be! A teachable person is someone you want to hire or even coach. You don't have to be the smartest person or the most gifted, but if you are teachable, you will go a long way in life!

From Doreen: I've seen the value of this in my life. I used to have very low self-confidence, so I would often get offended when someone corrected me. Proverbs is my favorite book in the Bible. As I began studying it more closely, I prayed to God for wisdom. He helped me, through His Word, be open to learning new things in every situation, while not being easily offended.

PRAYER:

Lord, in all my interactions today, may I be receptive to how I can grow and learn more about myself, You, and others. Amen.

CHALLENGE:

Humbly learn from the negative example of the fool's resistance.

_____
_____
_____

REBELLION

🌳 TODAY'S PASSAGE:

An evil man seeks only rebellion, and a cruel messenger will be sent against him. Let a man meet a she-bear robbed of her cubs rather than a fool in his folly.

Proverbs 17:11-12

COMMENTARY:

From Garry: The previous verse contrasted the person who was receptive to criticism with the fool who persisted in being closed-minded. This next set of verses takes it a step further. The persistent rebel will face the consequences. It might come as legal trouble or the consequences of his sin. Also, a warning is given about encountering a fool in his folly. He is unpredictable and even dangerous.

The following versions provide further explanations:

- "A disobedient person is only looking for trouble. So a cruel messenger will be sent against him. It is better to meet a bear robbed of her cubs than to meet a foolish person doing foolish things," (Proverbs 17:11-12 [ICB]).
- "Criminals out looking for nothing but trouble won't have to wait long—they'll meet it coming and going! Better to meet a grizzly robbed of her cubs than a fool hellbent on folly," (Proverbs 17:11-12 [MSG]).

From Ward: Generally speaking, I do not think of myself as a rebel. Yet sometimes, I will take action or say a word that does not follow God's rules. And that puts me in the class as a rebel. Why does a person want to rebel? Often, the primary reason is selfishness. The rebel believes his actions are justified to achieve his goal. Other people will rebel because they see persecution and injustice, and fight to establish a more equitable community.

The author of these two proverbs is thinking of the first type of rebel I mentioned. Too often, humans see life as a game of winners and losers. The winners have written the rules and retain power and influence for themselves. The rebels believe that no higher power can protect them, so they use whatever weapons they have to fight for what they believe is right. The weapons could be words or actions. But the rebel leaves God out of the planning. When I sin and rebel against God's law, it implies that I know better than Him and do not want His input at that very moment. Thankfully, God, my family, and my Christian friends will help me ask for forgiveness and repent.

How can we prevent rebellion against God? First, we must know what his rules are, like being patient, seeking good for others, and being willing to suffer. Second, we must commit our minds to following these rules. And third, we pray daily that we can follow our commitment. May all of us put rebellion in the background and let God lead us to right living.

From Cynthia: When we choose to interact or be with other people, we absorb their ways. We see it in families and friendships. The world judges us by the company we keep. Creating boundaries is difficult, but this passage is a wake-up call—to resist being with fools and embrace the Truth. I pray I am not foolish and that Christ is my witness when fools encounter me.

From Leslie: That's a serious analogy! Mama bear was robbed of her cubs. That's scary.

From Doreen: Sometimes fools can be intelligent and seem to have everything going for them. They can become so settled in their ways that they cannot recognize the need for change to achieve an even better, easier life.

PRAYER:

Lord, help me realize that sin has consequences. Father, protect me from wrong decisions and help me choose wisdom over folly. Amen.

CHALLENGE:

Open your eyes to Truth and the value of cooperation.

_____
_____
_____
_____
_____
_____
_____

NEVER RETURN EVIL FOR GOOD

 **TODAY'S PASSAGE:**

If anyone returns evil for good, evil will not depart from his house.

Proverbs 17:13

COMMENTARY:

From Garry: These are strong words. They point out the negative impact evil has and its consequences. They reveal something unnatural. When you are blessed with good, it makes little sense to respond with evil. Evil only makes things worse. Proverbs 17:13 (MSG) says, "Those who return evil for good will meet their own evil returning." Today's passage in Proverbs reminds me of what Paul wrote in Romans:

Repay no one evil for evil, but give thought to do what is honorable in the sight of all. If possible, so far as it depends on you, live peaceably with all. Beloved, never avenge yourselves, but leave it to the wrath of God, for it is written, "Vengeance is mine, I will repay, says the Lord." To the contrary, "if your enemy is hungry, feed him; if he is thirsty, give him something to drink; for by so doing, you will heap burning coals on his head." Do not be overcome by evil but overcome evil with good.

Romans 12:17-21 (ESV)

Another verse to remember is from 1 Peter:

Do not repay evil for evil or reviling for reviling, but on the contrary, bless, for to this you were called, that you may obtain a blessing. For "Whoever desires to love life and see good days, let him keep his tongue from evil and his lips from speaking deceit; let him turn away from evil and do good; let him seek

> *peace and pursue it. For the eyes of the Lord are on the righteous, and his ears are open to their prayer. But the face of the Lord is against those who do evil."*
> **1 Peter 3:9-12 (ESV)**

From Ward: Growing up as a shy child, I never had conflicts with other boys my age. I was uncoordinated in playing sports or other physical games, so I was not a threat to anyone. Boys my age who lost a game point and got angry would exclaim, "I'm going to get that other guy." Of course, all who heard these words knew that someone would possibly receive harm from the speaker. I was generally not passionate about any competition, so I did not understand why someone would plan revenge or evil against an opponent.

According to this proverb, many people are not like me. Winning, being number one, having their idea adopted, and receiving applause are important results of their work. For too many, evil tempts us to plot a way to harm, embarrass, or demean another. We cannot allow our minds to focus so intently on a loss that the only way to resolve our anger is to injure another.

Today, I am not a boy, and I think people now extend evil by using money and words. We should remember that our hands are for work and showing love. Our words are for communication and praising God. Our money is for spending, saving, and giving. These tools are not for manipulation, control, sowing discord, or seeking revenge. Those who sow evil will have evil intent live in their house. Those who continually focus on evil will eventually see their plans turn to dust.

Through forgiveness and repentance, we can purge evil from our house and allow love to reign in our minds. Let us always remember the godly use of our hands, our words, and our money, so that goodness may enter our front door and never leave our home.

From Wright: Garry, I like the way you use so much Scripture.

From Leslie:

> *In that while we were still sinners [His enemies], Christ died for us.*
> **Romans 5:8b (ESV, Emphasis Added)**

From John: Among all the people I have been around, the ones who live a negative lifestyle are the ones who seem to have the most difficulty in their lives. The negative lifestyle just permeates throughout their entire life.

From Jim: I had to think about this and examine my life. I preached on Revelation 21:1-8 last Sunday, connecting being a new creation to the future new heaven and new earth. As a person's accent and behavior reveal their nationality, our actions as Christians should clearly show our allegiance to God's kingdom, not the world. We are to bless those who curse us and to live out the fruit of the Spirit.

From Doreen: I would rather be blessed for being kind to a person who is mean to others, rather than being cursed for retaliating.

From Cindi: A beautiful response from a dear friend has stayed with me for years. She explained that they were driving on a congested highway when a motorist did not like that they slowed down to make the exit. From his horn, he gave them an offensive gesture and yelled something undoubtedly rude. Instead of responding to any of those mean things, the driver made the sign of the cross. May we all respond likewise! Send the light!

From Cynthia: I'm grateful when I'm speechless in the face of someone's words, because it's always tempting to return evil to those who are being evil. We are called to grow up and love all people in our actions and in how we express ourselves. We don't know what people are struggling with or how others can be hurt by our actions. I believe that is also why people are meant to face the consequences of their actions, so they can learn that evil must be stopped. I admire people who can de-escalate a situation with their words and actions of love.

PRAYER:

Lord, may I initiate goodness and blessing in what I say and do and turn away from every form of evil. Amen.

CHALLENGE:

In all your ways, do good, seek peace, and pursue it.

_____
_____
_____
_____
_____
_____
_____

STOP THE LEAK

 **TODAY'S PASSAGE:**

> *The beginning of strife is like letting out water, so quit before the quarrel breaks out.*
>
> **Proverbs 17:14**

COMMENTARY:

From Garry: Giving in to strife lets loose more than one can predict, control, or retrieve. Imagine a small leak in a large container. The water begins to spurt out. It will only get worse if it is not contained. Strife is like that.

> *The beginning of strife is like letting out water [as from a small break in a dam; first it trickles and then gushes]; Therefore abandon the quarrel before it breaks out and tempers explode.*
>
> **Proverbs 17:14 (AMP)**

> *The start of an argument is like a water leak—so stop it before real trouble breaks out.*
>
> **Proverbs 17 (CEV)**

In addition, there are similar Proverbs to today's passage:

- Proverbs 18:1 (ESV) says, "Whoever isolates himself seeks his own desire; he breaks out against all sound judgment."
- Proverbs 20:3 (ESV) says, "It is an honor for a man to keep aloof from strife, but every fool will be quarreling."

I also discovered that the Septuagint states, "The outpouring of words is the beginning of strife," (Proverbs 17:14 [LXX]). It warns us against careless talk. The issue is in recognizing strife and stopping it before it grows into a monster.

From Ward: Why is there strife between people? James 4:1b says in the Easy English Bible (EASY), "It is because of the troubles in your thoughts. You want to do bad things that you think will make you happy."

Joyce Meyer says the source of strife is coveting. I must admit, I do not think about coveting. And I do not remember ever asking God to forgive my sin of coveting. But we must all be tempted to do this, or else there would not be the tenth commandment.

Today's proverb reminds us it is better to stop strife at the beginning and not let it build into a deep quarrel. To achieve this, the members of the Body of Christ must be peacemakers. Paul says in Romans 12:18 (ESV), "If possible, so far as it depends on you, live peaceably with all." And Psalm 34:14b (ESV) says, "Seek peace and pursue it." Rather than looking for disagreement, we must seek peace and actively pursue it, not just hoping for peace to appear by chance.

How can we pursue peace? One saying on the internet is, "You do not have to attend every argument you are invited to." God may want us to participate in every discussion and try to convince every opponent to change. But we should pause when we speak and give our minds time to think rather than just reacting.

Lastly, we should try to understand the position and feelings of others. This is a challenging task, and I often struggle to accomplish it. However, I know it is necessary for peacemaking. I pray that all of us can undertake these actions and receive God's help to do them with sincerity and gentleness.

From Jim: This is one of those helpful verses to keep in mind and practice. Someone once asked me what my theology was for handling strife and quarreling. I believe every congregation and pastor should know what Scripture teaches us about this issue and how we should handle such matters. After putting this into practice and being willing to have such discussions with congregations, I find we are all better off, and life is much more peaceful. Even in my personal life, I strive to address such problems as soon as they arise, typically by discussing them with others. Thank you for this one.

From Cynthia: Our tone and our voice level determine how a conversation travels. The problem is that most people aren't aware of their contribution to the situation. Our lack of love, pride, and the need to be right keep us from doing the right thing. Seeing people through love keeps us from causing harm to others. No one wants to drown.

From Doreen: My life is more peaceful since I've worked on being less argumentative. It makes life better to be more positive instead of quarreling.

From Cindi: Let love for the other person be bigger than making a point, winning the argument, being right, or showing others how smart we are!

PRAYER:

Father, thank You that one of the fruits of the Spirit is self-control. May that be evident in my life in all my conversations, especially in the ones that are hard. Amen.

CHALLENGE:

When things get hot, have the courage to stop it right away.

_____
_____
_____
_____
_____
_____

JUSTICE AND INTEGRITY

 **TODAY'S PASSAGE:**

> *He who justifies the wicked and he who condemns the righteous are both alike an abomination to the LORD.*
>
> **Proverbs 17:15**

COMMENTARY:

From Garry: The New International Version translates today's passage as follows: "Acquitting the guilty and condemning the innocent—the LORD detests them both," (Proverbs 17:15 [NIV]). The Message Bible states it this way: "Whitewashing bad people and throwing mud on good people are equally abhorrent to GOD," (Proverbs 17:15 [MSG]).

God values the truth. God is a God of justice. When God's standards of justice and righteousness are upheld, there is equality, protection, freedom, and harmony. When justice is distorted, there are negative consequences. This proverb points out that God hates injustice because it causes disorder and confusion.

Justice and truth are valuable because they promote justice and hold us accountable. Social order and peace are built on truth. We honor God by reflecting truth and fairness in all our interactions. Truth and integrity cultivate a just and equitable society.

God's goal for creation is *shalom*. Biblical scholars from *The Institute For Faith, Work, and Economics* (https://tifwe.org/what-is-shalom-according-to-the-bible/) inform us that:

> Shalom signifies a number of things, including salvation, wholeness, integrity, soundness, community, connectedness (to others and to God's creation), righteousness, justice, and well-being (physical, psychological, and spiritual).

Today's Proverb warns against unjust judgments and their impact on both the innocent and the wicked.

From Ward: The word *abomination* is not one I typically use, and yet it appears in the Bible over 120 times in some versions. *Abomination* means disgusting, hateful, sinful, and wicked. Why does God find it so detestable to justify the wicked and condemn the righteous? Because this is the total opposite of God's character. These acts represent nothing that God is for.

1 Corinthians 5:9b (ESV) says, "We make it our aim to please him"—not to please ourselves or someone else. As believers in God, we have a duty to discern right from wrong and to support what is right while opposing what is wrong. Sometimes, responding correctly can cause loss, persecution, or death. However, when we allow wickedness to prevail and right living to falter, we permit evil to triumph.

God may allow evil to prevail for a time, but ultimately, God will defeat wrong. Like Garry wrote, I want to be on the side that honors God. Sustaining falsehood creates confusion and inequality. Ignoring wicked behavior to keep a calm environment will lead to the righteous being ignored and oppressed. We should take God's words seriously and proclaim His truth to the world. Jesus did this and called his disciples to follow Him. I often forget that following Jesus will cost me. I may lose friends, social standing, or wealth while being faithful. So, I remind myself that my commitment to God invites me to challenge the world's way of acting. Standing up for right living and condemning falsehood may not be easy, but this shows the world that I am on God's side. May all of us be willing to stand for what is right.

From John: In today's world, one constantly hears about people entering places of business and stealing items right off the shelves. Some communities do not hold these individuals accountable for their actions because of the dollar amount associated with that crime. Good, upright people suffer as a result. Throughout this country, people who have committed violent crimes are being released, and consequently, innocent people have lost their lives because of it. Christians must stand up against this type of justification of the wicked because if we do not stand for righteousness and accountability, then, as Christians, what do we stand for?

From Cindi: This verse causes me to offer prayers for our justice system, our education system, and all who have authority over our citizens. Introspectively, I pray the Lord will grant me discernment and wisdom so that I can share God's truth and love with others.

From Doreen: It's disheartening to see mean-spirited people show favoritism toward those who are evil and withhold kindness toward those who are good.

From Cynthia: We live in a world where the lines between right and wrong are often blurred, and people don't even know who they are. It is often a parent's role to help us find our identity amidst the confusion. Parents help us grow in the Lord when we need it most.

Take American philosopher Dallas Willard, for example. He left such a beautiful legacy pointing to Jesus, even though he lost his mother before his third birthday. Dallas' mother left behind poems and letters to her children during her last moments on earth. She hoped he would know Jesus, and the family made sure that he did. His attachment to his mother was so strong that he climbed into her casket during the wake when he was two and a half years old.

In Dallas Willard's last moments on earth, while dying of cancer, he said that Salvation—Jesus' saving grace—was the perfect example of a mother's love. We can all be forgiven of our imperfect parenting and offer Jesus' perfect love. Dallas W.'s last words were, "Thank you."

PRAYER:

Lord, You are the righteous judge of all the earth. Help me be honest and fair in my assessments of people and situations. Give me clarity. Help me be fair and walk in the Truth. Amen.

CHALLENGE:

God desires truth, righteousness, justice, and fairness in human institutions.

_____
_____
_____
_____
_____
_____
_____

A FOOL HAS NO SENSE

 **TODAY'S PASSAGE:**

Why should a fool have money in his hand to buy wisdom when he has no sense?

Proverbs 17:16

COMMENTARY:

From Garry: This proverb is an observation about the fool's incapacity to learn. The Hebrew term used for *fool* in this proverb is used 19 times in the Book of Proverbs. This term for *fool* suggests stupidity and stubbornness. He gives himself away as soon as he opens his mouth. He knows no restraint and has no sense of proportion.

- "It is senseless to pay to educate a fool, since he has no heart for learning," (Proverbs 17:16 [NLV]).
- "It won't do a fool any good to try to buy wisdom, because he doesn't have the ability to be wise," (Proverbs 17:16 [NCV]).

What good would it be to have money, since what the fool needs cannot be bought? Money would be wasted on a fool because the fool lacks heart and has no intention of acquiring wisdom.

- "Why should fools have money for an education when they refuse to learn," (Proverbs 17:16 [CEV])?
- "What's this? Fools out shopping for wisdom! They wouldn't recognize it if they saw it," (Proverbs 17:16 [MSG])!

From Ward: Have you ever bought wisdom? I do not remember paying money for wise words. My wisdom has come from listening to others wiser than myself and from my experiences. Trying to buy wisdom with money seems mindless. A fool is a person who has no regard for God or for other people. A fool believes he has all the education he needs, and along with his own skills and talents, any task can be accomplished. I wonder how often I act that way? Dear reader, please do not send me an email to answer that question. Thank you.

Adam and Eve were tempted by the same idea. They thought by eating the fruit of a certain tree, they would get all the knowledge they would need to make any future decisions. God wants us to rely on him, even when he has given us educational tools for dealing with struggles. 2 Corinthians 3:5b (NKJV) says, "Our sufficiency is from God." Education, wisdom, knowledge, and experience will not rescue us from the failings of this world. "Behold, God is my salvation," says Isaiah 12:2a (ESV). I want to remember this when I think I have all the answers. God has provided us with many solutions to the concerns of our life. Let us all acknowledge God as the source, not our own minds. Or else we will be like a fool who has no sense.

From Doreen: In my experience, fools just keep digging the hole they're in deeper and deeper, using a bigger shovel every time.

From Cindi: Math class was not my favorite as a youth, so I refused to learn as much as I could. This caught up with me in college! I had to work twice as hard! Lord, help me to never repeat foolish tendencies like this! Help me have a willing heart to learn what You have set before me!

From Cynthia: This is a judgmental message that can be interpreted in a couple of ways. I find it a warning to those who think "knowing things" or "having more money" will solve all their problems. It is also possible that appearances are more important to some people than the stewardship of time.

PRAYER:

Lord, I do not want to be foolish. I want to be wise. Help me, Lord! Amen.

CHALLENGE:

Have a humble and open heart for learning.

_____
_____
_____
_____
_____
_____
_____

A TRUE FRIEND

 **TODAY'S PASSAGE:**

A friend loves at all times, and a brother is born for adversity.

Proverbs 17:17

COMMENTARY:

From Garry: Two different versions of today's passage are:

- "A true friend is always there to love you, and family provides help when troubles come," (Proverbs 17:17 [FBV]).
- "A dear friend will love you no matter what, and a family sticks together through all kinds of trouble," (Proverbs 17:17 [TPT]). You can depend on a true friend because of their loyalty. They are constant and trustworthy.

Two other passages in Proverbs that address friendship are:

- "Friends come and friends go, but a true friend sticks by you like family," (Proverbs 18:24 [MSG]). A true friend is honest with you.
- "Faithful are the wounds of a friend, but the kisses of an enemy are deceitful," (Proverbs 27:6 [MEV]). A true friend offers good counsel.

A true friend shows respect for your feelings. He uses tact and is kind and generous. I am so thankful to God for the friends I have. I am also so thankful for my family. If I were in trouble, they'd go to any lengths to assist me.

From Ward: How do you define being a friend? Take a moment and write down words and phrases on the lines at the end of this devotion. I looked on the Internet for random definitions of what it means to be a friend, and here are some responses:

- Few and far between, rare.
- Having a deep relationship that has been built over time.
- Empathy and mutual support.
- I can be myself with this person.
- A cheerleader for you, no judgments.
- The person will always be there for you.
- You can share your deepest thoughts with this person.
- It is easy to be with each other.
- If we have not seen each other for a time, we can pick up where we left off.
- They love you.
- They do not disappear.
- You feel like they are family.

Friendships are crucial to our well-being. Jesus treats us this way. God treats us this way. No one mentioned receiving advice, gifts, or money, even though these things often happen among friends. The intangibles of friendships are more important than the tangibles. Let us do these same actions with the people we know, which results in God being glorified in this world.

From Frank: Amen. Beautiful, Garry. And I am blessed you are my friend and brother.

From Doreen: Close friends can help make life easier when going through a tough time. Sometimes, it's easier to talk to a friend than to family. Having a close family member present during a difficult time is a blessing.

From Cynthia: Healthy friendships help us build character and prepare us for a joyous life. I'm grateful to be blessed with friends who love the Truth.

PRAYER:

Father, thank You for sending Jesus Christ to be our Friend, as well as our Brother. We can certainly depend on Him! Amen.

CHALLENGE:

Be a true friend by being like Jesus.

_____
_____
_____
_____
_____
_____

PRUDENCE AND PROMISES

 **TODAY'S PASSAGE:**

> *One who lacks sense gives a pledge and puts up security in the presence of his neighbor.*
>
> **Proverbs 17:18**

COMMENTARY:

From Garry: Today's passage is a reminder of Proverbs 6:1-5:

> *My son, if you have put up security for your neighbor, have given your pledge for a stranger, if you are snared in the words of your mouth, caught in the words of your mouth, then do this, my son, and save yourself, for you have come into the hand of your neighbor: go, hasten, and plead urgently with your neighbor. Give your eyes no sleep and your eyelids no slumber; save yourself like a gazelle from the hand of the hunter, like a bird from the hand of the fowler.*
>
> **Proverbs 6:1-5 (ESV)**

In other words, if you make a rash promise, keep it. Make it good. Learn not to make such promises in the first place. Don't promise to pay someone else's debt. Avoid making rash promises and getting yourself into trouble. Use self-control. The Good News Translation says, "Only someone with no sense would promise to be responsible for someone else's debts," (Proverbs 17:18 [GNT]). This Proverb is like a favorite quote of a close friend and longtime mentor: "No one has the moral right to make someone else responsible for their happiness."

From Ward:
We often have empathy for the struggles a friend has, and we long to assist. But being a guarantor for another person's debt is not the help that should be given. Too often, the debtor is nowhere to be found when the debt is due, so the guarantor ends up paying the debt. Everyone should work to pay the debts they owe. It is fine to offer to pay a part or all of a person's debt by paying directly to the creditor. Being a guarantor or giving the money directly to the debtor is not wise, however.

Not all people we know are honest and truthful about their finances. We should not lose *our* savings to eliminate someone else's debt. Our concern for others includes encouraging them to bear the responsibility for the solution to their crisis.

Paul, in Galatians 6 (NKJV), tells us to "bear each other's burdens," but that "each one should bear their own load." We should ask God for discernment in knowing what is a *burden* and what is a *load f*or our neighbor. Confusing the two may lead to our own financial crisis. May God grant us sympathy so we can be kind and self-controlled but not swayed by a heartbreaking story.

From Leslie: When my husband worked at the bank, he always cautioned people before co-signing a loan. He would warn them of the risks and clearly explain their commitment.

From John: A long time ago, I was taught not to give a pledge or co-sign a note for anyone unless you wanted the item your pledge guaranteed. Essentially, without going through personal hardships, I learned that the person who could not get something with his resources did not need that item. Amazing what I was taught as a young man came from Proverbs 17:18.

From Doreen: Loaning to others has caused long-term trouble for several people that I know. In my opinion, if a person lacks the credit to be approved for a loan, others should be cautious in co-signing with them.

From Cynthia: I've been on both sides of this financial mistake. There are times when someone is drowning in debt, and God may direct us to assist. There are other times when

He wants them to see that there is something in their life blocking His blessing, such as refusing to work, or to live within their means. When it comes to finances we must all pray to God for the right path to financial freedom, and there are many paths that benefit everyone.

PRAYER:

Lord, give me prudence regarding financial decisions. May I exercise self-control, and be careful. I know it is good to be generous, but being wise in the process is important. Amen.

CHALLENGE:

Use good judgment and avoid rash decisions.

_____
_____
_____
_____
_____
_____
_____

BUILD A BRIDGE, NOT A WALL

 **TODAY'S PASSAGE:**

Whoever loves transgression loves strife; he who makes his door high seeks destruction.

Proverbs 17:19

COMMENTARY:

From Garry: This proverb describes an arrogant person who causes problems in relationships. Consider these versions:

- "To like sin is to like making trouble. If you brag all the time, you are asking for trouble," (Proverbs 17:19 [GNT]).
- "The person who courts sin marries trouble; build a wall, invite a burglar," (Proverbs 17:19 [MSG]).
- "The one who loves a quarrel loves transgression, whoever builds his gate high seeks destruction," (Proverbs 17:19 [NET]). The gate is the mouth, and to make it high is to speak loftily—he brags too much.

What a contrast to what Jesus taught in his Sermon on the Mount: "Blessed are those who hunger and thirst for righteousness, for they will be filled," (Matthew 5:6 [NIV]).

From Ward: What do you seek? What outcomes do you want? Please take a moment and use the lines at the end of this devotion to write some words about what you seek. Are these goals the same as 10 years ago? Or when you were a teen? Probably not all your desires are the same. One meaning of love is having a commitment to a person, idea, or action. In this proverb, the author tells us that those who are committed to transgression are also committed to strife. Wow, what a stressful life this must be! I would not want to be a person who was continually linked to conflict. Yet some people, as they see this, aim to develop power and influence over others.

Jesus did not act this way. He showed us that having goals like kindness, patience, sincerity, and compassion helped us accomplish our goals better than being self-centered. The apostle Paul tells us in 2 Corinthians 5:9 that we make it our aim to please God (my paraphrase). In Romans 12:18, we should pursue peace with all (my paraphrase). In Joshua 1:7, Joshua tells the people that if they obey the rules that Moses wrote, they will have success in all their work (my paraphrase). I encourage you, as you think about your goals, to pursue them without causing conflict. You will have an easier time achieving them and will have less stress.

From Jim: Today's passage is interesting. I had not considered "making your door high" in this sense of bragging. Yet it makes sense. This verse implies that I am elevating myself above others. Lord, help me seek humbleness and humility.

From Kyle: There are those that I know who love to argue. Pick the subject, pick the position, and they will take the opposite approach, as they love a good argument. I know others who also get satisfaction from being angry, from unleashing their temper.

Some believe that if you are angry because someone hurt you or sinned against you, then your anger is righteous. But not so. The website, *A Place of Hope* (https://www.aplaceofhope.com/resolving-anger-the-proverbs-series-protection-or-destruction-proverbs-1719/) explains it this way:

> Even if the source of your anger comes from sin committed against you, that does not absolve you from responsibility in how you conduct yourself and express your anger. [If you were allowed to be angry for a valid reason with no fault to how you reacted, then you could abuse and be free from guilt.] No one would be held responsible for their own wrongful actions because [they had] been wronged by [another].

In order to heal and get over your anger, you need to start seeing it in its proper context—as a high gate you've built for protection. As this verse cautions, though a high gate does provide protection, it also invites destruction. If you doubt that, just think about the effect your anger has on those you love."

Ask yourself—is your anger protecting or destroying your family relationships?

From Doreen: In my experience, people who are arrogant and/or love conflict often feel like they're right, regardless of what anyone says. They don't realize how annoying they are. If someone holds them accountable, they become annoyed and act as if the other person has done something wrong.

From Cynthia: Could this include those who live beyond their means? We are in this world for a season, to bring Glory to God and to resist "drama." We are to avoid impressing others with our material goods.

From Frank: It aligns with the idea of reaping what we sow (Galatians 6:7-8), doesn't it? Jesus further states in the Sermon on the Mount, as recorded in Matthew 5:1-11 (paraphrased), that the merciful shall obtain mercy, the meek shall inherit the earth, and the peacemakers shall be called the children of God. If we pick a fight, we will find one; if we seek the Lord, He will find us.

From Cindi: Lord, keep my discussions from being arguments. Please help me be mindful of my speech so that I do not give the impression of being overly confident.

PRAYER:

Father, help me be humble in my speech. Amen.

CHALLENGE:

Love God, love people, and break down the walls.

OUR HEART'S CONDITION

 TODAY'S PASSAGE:

A man of crooked heart does not discover good, and one with a dishonest tongue falls into calamity.

Proverbs 17:20

COMMENTARY:

From Garry: Here is a warning that trouble comes to us when our heart is not right. In this proverb, "heart" and "tongue" are linked. The heart involves the mind and the will, which affect all our actions. The condition of our heart affects our speech. Jesus taught that every good tree bears good fruit, and every bad tree bears bad fruit. Jesus also taught that it is out of the heart that the mouth speaks.

As I thought about the heart, I asked myself, "How do the Proverbs speak about the heart?" Proverbs 3:1-4 emphasizes the importance of letting your heart keep the commandments and the significance of inscribing steadfast love and faithfulness on the tablet of your heart. When you do, good things happen. Other scriptures to consider are:

- Proverbs 3:5-6 (ESV) says, "Trust in the LORD with all your heart, and do not lean on your own understanding. In all your ways acknowledge him, and he will make straight your paths."
- Proverbs 10:8 (ESV) says, "The wise of heart will receive commandments, but a babbling fool will come to ruin."
- Proverbs 4:23-24 (ESV) says, "Keep your heart with all vigilance, for from it flow the springs of life. Put away from you crooked speech, and put devious talk far from you."

Consider the condition of your heart. Is it hindering your ability to speak and negatively affecting your life's outcome?

From Ward: Why is there dishonesty? Possibly fear, a desire to gain an advantage over someone, a wish to avoid discipline, a reluctance to avoid an argument, or it may be easier than telling a long story that is true. What does dishonesty lead to? Confusion, going in the wrong direction, lack of trust, and a tarnished reputation. Dishonesty is rampant in our culture today. Some folks believe that much of today's advertising is misleading and not straightforward. My judgment is that many companies achieve significant profits through deception and continue to operate for many years. If deception is such a part of our public communication, why do we not see the conclusion of this proverb: "One with a dishonest tongue falls into calamity," (Proverbs 17:20b [ESV])?

Our culture accepts, and might even encourage, dishonesty as a standard procedure for accomplishing work and service. The latest Gallup survey finds that only 32 percent of Americans find pastors trustworthy. Today, no one loudly proclaims against deception. There is no higher authority now to discourage this practice and enforce integrity. What can be our response? As individuals, we have little power to enforce honesty in the workplace and in others.

What we can do is choose integrity. In Joshua 24, Joshua speaks to the people. He tells them to fear the Lord faithfully and to throw out all objects related to foreign gods. He continues by saying, "If you do not want to serve God, then you must choose whom to serve." Joshua concludes that each family will need to decide, but for his household, "we will serve the Lord" (Joshua 24:15b [NIV]).

As Christians, we can make a choice for right living for ourselves and hope that others will follow our example. We can also pray that those with power and influence will see the error of continual deception and choose to follow the path of Jesus. In Isaiah 53:9b (NIV), when the author predicts Jesus' life, he writes, "There was no deceit in his mouth." Let each one of us choose honest and polite speech in all our conversations.

From Cynthia: People are gravitating either towards God—or away from God. It matters who or what we are listening to because we are conditioning our hearts and preparing for what we are interested in. Psalm 51:10, a beloved Scripture, reminds us to ask God to condition our hearts and make straight the way for Jesus.

From Leslie: Additional scriptures to consider are Luke 6:45, Mark 7:21, and Jeremiah 17:9. I loved your prayer, Garry. God must make us new.

From Doreen: If you have a crooked heart, you may have lived a hard life. There are likely resultant issues with anger, impatience, and unforgiveness, which could lead to health concerns, as well.

From Frank: This is so powerful. If the heart isn't right, and the tongue that is not controlled spews trouble, then calamity finds its way into your life.

From Jim: After preaching from Hebrews this month, I am of the mind that human beings have a heart condition. Is it not telling that in the new covenant, God will take out our heart of stone and give us a heart of flesh? Oh, that His commands will be placed in our minds and written on our hearts.

From Barrett: Especially given recent days, Proverbs 3:5-6 has resonated with me:

> *Trust in the LORD with all your heart and do not lean on your own understanding. In all your ways acknowledge Him, and He will make straight your paths.*
>
> **Proverbs 3:5-6 (ESV)**

When you rely on your own understanding—your intellect, logic, and faculties—worldly desires will draw you away from God's Truth and prevent you from seeing *His* ways in your heart. On the other hand, when you open your heart, you will see that logic will drag you toward God's Truth, not away from it. What was a hindrance becomes furtherance and facilitation. The ability to listen is a rare talent; the ability to hear is an even more cherished ability. To God belongs our worship for His Glory.

PRAYER:

Lord, create in me a clean heart and renew a right spirit within me. Amen.

CHALLENGE:

When your heart is not right, there will be problems.

_____
_____
_____
_____
_____
_____
_____
_____

FOOLS MESS UP LIFE

 **TODAY'S PASSAGE:**

He who sires a fool gets himself sorrow, and the father of a fool has no joy.
Proverbs 17:21

COMMENTARY:

From Garry: This proverb uses the term *fool* twice. But the Hebrew words are different. The first Hebrew term for *fool* describes a person who is stupid. Words that describe him are airhead, birdbrain, blockhead, and knucklehead in almost all matters of life, whether spiritual, intellectual, or moral matters. This term for *fool* is used fifty times in Proverbs.

The second term for *fool* in this verse is only used three times in the Book of Proverbs. It describes a person whose mind is closed to God and to reason. It is a *fool* who is ill-mannered or insensitive. Other similar proverbs from the English Standard Version are:

- Proverbs 17:25 (ESV) says, "A foolish son is a grief to his father and bitterness to her who bore him."
- Proverbs 10:1 (ESV) states, "A wise son makes a glad father, but a foolish son is a sorrow to his mother."
- Proverbs 15:20 (ESV) says, "A wise son makes a glad father, but a foolish man despises his mother."

The father of a fool experiences grief, bitterness, and sorrow. But joy is for the father of a wise son.

From Ward: Think of some of the choices you have made in your life. Please jot them down at the end of this devotion. Were the choices major or minor? Would you have made the same choices today as you did in the past? Did you find all the options useful?

We may not realize this, but being a fool in the Biblical meaning is a choice. If you are living a life without thinking about God, without thinking of the future, and without thinking about your effect on others, then the person stops, acts as if God does not exist, and believes he is the source of all goodness for himself. This type of person brings sorrow to his family because he ignores the input of others and relies on his own imagination. His worth is not influenced by his parents, so his family has little joy in a relationship with him. This must be a lonely life being on top of the hill with few people beside you, except for "Yes" men.

Reaching out to others for wisdom and help is not a mark of weakness. Today, too many people believe that all great ideas are unique to them, come from an individual's mind, and are not based on the previous achievements of others. A Biblical fool's disregard for contemplating past events and facts makes the path to success long, bumpy, and slow, with a strong possibility of failure. May all of us be humble so we can acknowledge our dependence on both God and all the wise people in our community who can keep us on the path to right living.

From Frank: Amen! This is insightful, Garry. Thanks for taking the time to do this interesting word study.

From Cindi: However, she who has sensible, loving children gets herself much joy! I am so thankful for my three young adult children who are not foolish. My own youthful foolishness has been forgiven by the blood of Jesus Christ. Apparently, I had enough foolishness for my whole family.

From Cynthia: Wouldn't it be a great Sunday School/Kids Church lesson to teach preschool and kindergarten children about boundaries and how to bring joy to their parents? The media and advertisements, busy schedules, and phones are rapidly disconnecting our relationships. Music, games, sports, and books connect us. People who thrive in their relationships have invested time with those who care about them. Family Time=Love.

PRAYER:

Lord, foolishness creates all kinds of problems. May I stay away from it in all its forms. Amen.

CHALLENGE:

Foolish living really messes things up.

___
___
___
___
___
___
___

REJOICE! BE GLAD!

TODAY'S PASSAGE:

A joyful heart is good medicine, but a crushed spirit dries up the bones.
                                                            Proverbs 17:22

COMMENTARY:

From Garry: Think about the previous verse, how the father of a fool has no joy. Now, this proverb describes how a joyful heart brings healing. Joy is good for your health! Joy in our hearts is like medicine. A cheerful attitude is good for our health. Sometimes, we can let circumstances determine our disposition. They can affect the way we think. But the Bible says: "Rejoice!" In fact, it says, "Rejoice always!"

In the English Standard Version, several Proverbs contrast a heart that is joyful with a heart that is struggling.

- "Anxiety in a man's heart weighs him down, but a good word makes him glad," (Proverbs 12:25 [ESV]).
- "A glad heart makes a cheerful face, but by sorrow of heart the spirit is crushed," (Proverbs 15:13 [ESV]).
- "All the days of the afflicted are evil, but the cheerful of heart has a continual feast," (Proverbs 15:15 [ESV]).
- "A man's spirit will endure sickness, but a crushed spirit who can bear," (Proverbs 18:14 [ESV])?

As I journaled about Proverbs 17:22, I wrote:

Joyful Heart → Good Medicine
Good Word → Makes Him Glad

  Glad Heart → Has a Cheerful Face
  Cheerful Heart → Has a Continual Feast
  Crushed Spirit → Dries Up Bones
  Anxious Heart → Weighed Down
  Sorrowful Heart → Spirit Crushed
  Crushed Spirit → Who Can Bear?

From Ward: A 2021 Harvard Medical Study concluded, "People who describe themselves as happy tend to have fewer health problems, a lower risk of depression, and longer lives." A *2023 Scripps News* article mentions research showing that happier people have higher antibody responses to vaccines, lower blood pressure and heart rates, and are less likely to suffer from chronic pain. So, this proverb is correct. Nehemiah 8:10b (NKJV) says, "For the joy of the Lord is our strength."

  But not everyone is happy. Challenging circumstances can make it difficult to find any joy. Happiness can be learned and developed. We cannot manufacture happiness, but we can use techniques that increase positive emotions inside us. These skills include practicing being thankful. Reflect on and appreciate the good aspects of your life, focusing on the positives and the accomplishments you've made. Next, be aware of your desires and do not let them overwhelm you. Lastly, manage your physical health by getting enough sleep, eating healthy food, and exercising. All these efforts can increase your ability to be happy.

  There is an abundance of negative news around us each day. Do not let those events steal our joy. Lord, help us develop a positive attitude that brings health to our bodies and peace to the surrounding community.

From Frank: Amen!

From Myra: Such good, wise words from our Lord. Your summary, Garry, is something to frame and exhibit in our home. I recall the story in Acts 16:25-34, where, even in prison, Paul and Silas sang and prayed. "About midnight, Paul and Silas were praying and singing hymns to God, and the other prisoners were listening to them" (Acts 16:25 [NIV]). I equate singing to a joyful spirit. This spiritual example teaches us what to expect when we exhibit a joyful, trusting spirit in the Lord—God hears us, others hear, and God acts.

From Doreen: I'm going through a period of healing, and I'm unable to work out with weights or go rock climbing. I enjoy both activities immensely and feel they are important. There have been a few times when I've been discouraged about it. In those times, I've had to rebuke negative thoughts and put on some upbeat music to help my mood.

In recent years, I've made an effort to smile more, help others, and offer compliments to people. Sometimes, this can turn someone's mood around, perhaps even their life. We never know if someone has a crushed spirit.

Some friends of ours moved recently. They are a very busy couple with elderly parents and a busy extended family. I offered to help them pack and unpack. A few weeks after they moved, my friend told me she needed my emotional support during that time because she was so overwhelmed. I had been able to help her unpack and listen to her vent. She said that my presence that day helped her turn a corner and feel better.

She and her husband are long-distance cyclists. Due to the busyness of the move, she was unable to go bike riding. I told her she needed to ride in her neighborhood, if nothing else, because she was missing something that gave her happiness. The following weekend, they went riding with some other friends. The difference in her mood the next time we saw her was noticeable. I do my best to remember that it's okay to enjoy your life when you're going through a struggle.

From Cindi: Amen! Lord, show me joy in all circumstances! Let us reflect Your light!

From Cynthia: Teachers, ministers, coaches, parents, grandparents, and others—everyone has the power to influence with just a word, a look, or a prayer. When we are grateful and our words are encouraging, we are furthering the kingdom of God by being joyful.

PRAYER:

Lord, you made us and have blessed us. We have so much to be thankful for! An attitude of joy blesses us and blesses those around us. Help us have a heart of joy! Amen.

CHALLENGE:

Rejoice in the Lord! Again, I say, rejoice!

_____
_____
_____
_____
_____
_____
_____

GREED

 **TODAY'S PASSAGE:**

The wicked accepts a bribe in secret to pervert the ways of justice.

Proverbs 17:23

COMMENTARY:

From Garry: The Passion Translation says, "When you take a secret bribe, your actions reveal your true character, for you pervert the ways of justice" (Proverbs 17:23 [TPT]). Why would a person accept a bribe in secret? It must be a hidden thing so others will not know. It also perverts the ways of justice.

Greed is wrong. Greed is an excessive desire for more money or possessions. Greed is the desire for more material gain or social status. Greed can lead to all sorts of wrong behavior: hoarding, overspending, or even gambling or theft. The love of money is the root of all kinds of evil.

- Ephesians 5:5 (NIV) says, "For of this you can be sure: No immoral, impure or greedy person—such a person is an idolater—has any inheritance in the kingdom of Christ and of God."
- Hebrews 13:5 (ESV) says, "Keep your life free from love of money, and be content with what you have, for he has said, "I will never leave you nor forsake you."

From Ward: Are you ever greedy? Do you know a person who is greedy or willing to take a bribe? We should never seek to twist a circumstance to produce only good for us. This is what a bribe attempts to do. Asking for a bribe is on the taking side of life. Jesus wants us on the giving side of life. For example, in the gospel of John (NIV version), Jesus says the word "give" at least 28 times and the word "take" only six times. I believe that if there is a choice in a circumstance of taking or giving, it is wiser to be a giving person.

I do not think of myself as greedy or demanding for money. But I wonder if I ever try to bribe God. Do I try to make a deal with God, insisting that if I pray a certain amount of time or do a good deed, God owes me a "Yes" answer to a prayer? We should not negotiate with God, for He is the author of grace and owes us nothing. Psalm 85:12a (NIV) says, "The LORD will indeed give what is good." God wants us to seek him for abundance and not use crooked schemes to enrich ourselves.

Psalm 36:7b-8a (NKJV) says, "The children of men...are abundantly satisfied with the fullness of Your [God's] house" [Emphasis Added]. Our work and our efforts should bring success to our family and not pervert justice. We should teach our children not to accept a bribe and be an example of that in our own lives.

From Frank: Amen! Greed can be so subtle and insidious.

From Leslie: I agree, Garry.

From Cindi: I was once a part of a mission trip to Peru. While the elders met in the church, I was helping to watch the children play outside. The dozens of kids played soccer with a very beat-up, half-deflated ball. Not one child cried, whined, argued, or tried to keep it for themselves. They were so joyful and content. It was beautiful! Coming home to the land of plenty and listening to our children relate to each other in a room full of toys was very different! We must teach our children to be content and generous. Are we focusing our families on relationships and generosity? Are we good examples of contentment? Lord, show us how to refocus!

From Doreen: As I've stated previously, bribery happens daily in my industry. It grieves me when greedy leaders are swayed by lobbyists' bribes to pass laws that hurt other people.

From Cynthia: We lead abundant lives, and we need to trust God so we can be generous to others. Jesus gave us everything we need. Jesus *is* everything we need. One day, I want my life to point only to Jesus.

PRAYER:

Lord, guard my heart from greed. Help me be content and understand Your call for me to be generous rather than greedy. Amen.

CHALLENGE:

Understand that contentment leads to peace.

WISDOM RIGHT IN FRONT OF YOU

 TODAY'S PASSAGE:

> *The discerning sets his face toward wisdom, but the eyes of a fool are on the ends of the earth.*
>
> **Proverbs 17:24**

COMMENTARY:

From Garry: Here are two other versions of this proverb:

- The New Living Translation says: "Sensible people keep their eyes glued on wisdom, but a fool's eyes wander to the ends of the earth," (Proverbs 17:24 [NLT]).
- The Message Bible says, "The perceptive find wisdom in their own front yard; fools look for it everywhere but right here," (Proverbs 17:24 [MSG]).

In reflecting on this proverb, I can visualize two people. One is focused, confident, and clear-headed. You can trust what he says. He is pure, peaceable, gentle, and open to reason. He is full of mercy and is impartial and sincere. The other person is someone you cannot trust because he is scatterbrained. He is arrogant and overly confident. You never know what he will say next. He is indecisive, and his divided loyalties reveal a life that is unfocused. As I think about this verse, what comes to mind is a verse in James:

> *If any of you lacks wisdom, let him ask God, who gives generously to all without reproach, and it will be given him. But let him ask in faith, with no doubting, for the one who doubts is like a wave of the sea that is driven and tossed by the*

> *wind. For that person must not suppose that he will receive anything from the LORD; he is a double-minded man, unstable in all his ways.*
>
> **James 1:5-8 (ESV)**

Those who are discerning are clear about who they are in the eyes of God. A faithful person is focused, in contrast to the fool who wanders aimlessly.

From Ward: Some people do not want to change their opinion. I think some folks ignore wisdom because it is too tough to think in a new way. I encourage you to think about any opinions or ideas that you now hold that you did not have five years ago, ten years ago, or longer. If a thought comes to your mind, write it on the lines at the end of this devotion. Have any of these new thoughts changed how you view the world? Did any of these thoughts change the way you acted or how you treated others?

Maybe some readers have had no opinion or concept changes in the last few years. I believe that is OK; however, this proverb, in Hebrew, tells us that wisdom stands in front of the person who wants understanding. This means as I seek to be wise, I can expect God to show me wisdom. The writers of all these proverbs expect a person to gather wisdom as we age. This means we may expand or modify our ideas and sometimes let go of them as wisdom is revealed.

William Arthur Ward wrote, "The pessimist complains about the wind; the optimist expects it to change; the realist adjusts the sails." Our world will change in the future, and we should be prepared. To look at the earth with the eyes of today and expect no real change in the future is part of being a fool. Having a significant life experience without reinforcing or changing your thoughts, ideas, or behavior is to lose the benefits of the experience.

Wisdom is available to all people, and God wants us to seek it. Living life by focusing solely on what makes us happy allows us to bypass learning wisdom and avoid understanding. May we all value wisdom more than the temporary pleasures of this world.

From Doreen: In my younger years, I did many foolish things—mainly because I was young and immature, and my faith was not as strong as it is now. Thankfully, I gained a lot of wisdom from those choices. I have also gained more wisdom from studying, praying, and observing others make foolish mistakes. The Lord was indeed watching over me in my younger years and helped guide me back to a better life.

Making Bible study a habit and learning to listen to the guidance of the Holy Spirit has been tremendously helpful. I can honestly see that a life away from God and Christian people is a foolish way of life.

From Cynthia: Discerning is the key word here. The same events that can turn a heart to Jesus can also cause people to run in the opposite direction. Our hearts and minds need to be discerning when we study the Bible and when we worship. Discernment truly is a gift to accept from God.

PRAYER:

Lord, You are the source of wisdom. May I look to You and stay focused on living a faithful life. Amen.

CHALLENGE:
Look to God, the Author of wisdom.

_____
_____
_____
_____
_____
_____

THE PAIN FOOLISH LIVING CREATES

 **TODAY'S PASSAGE:**

A foolish son is a grief to his father and bitterness to her who bore him.
Proverbs 17:25

COMMENTARY:

From Garry: Some proverbs are repeated over and over. Maybe that is because the author wanted to stress the importance of the family being wise. A family that honors God is a blessing to the community. A family that honors God experiences joy and spreads peace. A family that loves God and promotes his ways persistently provides direction and fosters wise habits of thought and action. There is open communication and appreciation, mutual respect, active listening, and forgiveness.

However, the father of a fool experiences grief because foolish living creates numerous problems. Foolish living creates misunderstanding and strife because it ignores the fear of the Lord. It chooses arrogance and self-centered living, which brings chaos and destruction.

But joy is for the father of a wise son. Proverbs 10:1(ESV) says, "A wise son makes a glad father, but a foolish son is a sorrow to his mother." Proverbs 15:20 (ESV) says, "A wise son makes a glad father, but a foolish man despises his mother." The mother of a fool, on the other hand, experiences sorrow, heartache, and bitterness.

From Ward: Do you have a relative or good friend who repeats a certain truth often? Sometimes, so often, you want to say the words at the same time as the other person. The writers of Proverbs have the same habit, contrasting wisdom with foolishness. Sometimes, the same images are repeated. Why? I believe the authors want us to remember and never forget the significance of being wise.

Zig Ziglar once wrote, "Repetition is the mother of learning, the father of action, which makes it the architect of accomplishment." John Wooden wrote, "The eight laws of learning are explanation, demonstration, imitation, repetition, repetition, repetition, repetition, repetition." He also wrote, "Repetition is the key to learning."

As much as I grow tired of reading the same idea several times, I know that repetition prevents me from making the same mistake repeatedly. None of us can remember every word that has been spoken to us or every word we have read. As we tie the truths of living to our experiences, we have a better chance of remembering the lessons. And if we have friends and family that are close, we can share those lessons with them.

None of us live totally alone. Even a hermit must eat what he plants. We should not let any harshness in our upbringing allow us to focus solely on negative lessons. Wisdom may be deeply hidden amid oppression and abuse, but God still loves us. Jesus still redeems our past and offers release to the captives.

New life in a relationship with God is available, as we do not allow foolishness to be our guide and captor. May the Father grant us strength to release any foolishness we may have adopted so we may claim His wisdom.

From Leslie: "The fear of the LORD is the beginning of wisdom" (Proverbs 9:10a [ESV]). Parents who respect God will try to teach their children the same. The family certainly benefits from it in many ways.

From Doreen: I know some people who are living this Bible verse out right now, and it's hard to watch. Being raised in a Bible-based church doesn't mean you won't make mistakes. But, hopefully, you learn from the mistakes you and those around you make. That's how you gain wisdom. Constantly making the same mistakes can be life-altering.

From Cindi: Parenting is challenging, but the effort is worthwhile! As a former teacher, I know how very much the children need parenting, not placating! I pray for wisdom and for the Lord's guidance for parents.

From Cynthia: There is so much advice on how to raise children that sometimes we ignore it all. Perhaps, when you think parenting is going along smoothly, it suddenly falls apart. Problems may arise that require intervention and outside resources. Foolish mistakes are costly. One foolish decision can put the rest of your life on a bleak trajectory. Ultimately, we give honor to our mother and father through the actions and decisions we make.

PRAYER:

Lord, help our family glorify you by choosing wisdom over foolishness. Amen.

CHALLENGE:

Honor your father and mother, that it might go well with you.

_____
_____
_____
_____
_____
_____
_____

FAIR JUDGMENT

 **TODAY'S PASSAGE:**

To impose a fine on a righteous man is not good, nor to strike the noble for their uprightness.

Proverbs 17:26

COMMENTARY:

From Garry: Here are two other versions of this proverb:

- The Message Bible says, "It's wrong to penalize good behavior, or make good citizens pay for the crimes of others," (Proverbs 17:26 [MSG]).
- The Contemporary English Version says, "It isn't fair to punish the innocent and those who do right," (Proverbs 17:26 [CEV]).

God is a God of justice. God is disgusted when legal verdicts are perverted for the wrong reasons. In Proverbs 17: 8, 13 and 23, the reader is warned against the bribe for personal gain or actions taken to satisfy greed. God is not pleased with injustice. Proverbs 17:15 (ESV) says, "He who justifies the wicked and he who condemns the righteous are both alike an abomination to the LORD."

God is a God of justice, and He watches human affairs to see whether hearts and words live up to the standards of love and justice. God wants the truth. When the truth is distorted, there are all kinds of problems.

From Ward: In ancient Israel, most persons convicted of a crime were not sent to prison. Prison was used for those awaiting execution or as a punishment for the very poor. Those who were not abjectly poor would pay a fine. Occasionally, government leaders would use the threat of prison and paying a fine to control local citizens. This proverb reminds leaders not to charge the righteous with crimes that have not happened and not to use physical violence against the innocent. God's desire is to protect the poor and powerless, not for the boss to use them to display his authority.

When our national government was established, the founders created a system that allowed leadership to change regularly. Too often, this has not happened and elected government officials have served many years. God's plan is for the righteous to rule by being just leaders. But we live in a sinful world, so leaders are tempted and yield to corruption of their power to enrich themselves and their friends. Our duty as Christians is to pray that God will allow righteous and just men and women to come forward to lead our nation at all levels. And they would not be tempted to misuse their power.

Our nation has fewer people now than previously, who acknowledge God has any involvement in or directives for our current life. Declining religious participation in worship or those who confess a personal relationship with God, makes finding righteous leaders who put God first unlikely here.

But we do not give up hope. God, our Father, is still the ruler of the universe and he can make the righteous reign if we do not give up praying for this. Establishing righteousness in our government at all levels is not an impossible result. I encourage you to pray daily for the next year that godly men and women would be in all avenues of leadership, so that justice and peace may happen in our nation.

Paul, in 1 Timothy 2:1-4, writes that we should first offer prayers for kings and people in authority. Thus, we may lead a peaceful life and provide our community with the ability and opportunity for all to be saved. This may be the most important prayer for our nation for the next decade. James 5:16b (ESV) says, "The prayer of a righteous person has great power as it is working." Let us who believe righteous behavior is a necessary part of a successful community pray for this to happen.

From Cindi: Lord, help us see what is true and just. Keep us from being indifferent to injustice and show us Your Truth. Give me courage to speak Your Truth and help me help those who are suffering.

From Cynthia: Where is the line between right and wrong in our world today? Without God, there *is* no moral compass. We hope our lives point other people toward Jesus. Thank God that the government is on His shoulders.

PRAYER:

Lord, I realize we live in a world where injustice happens. Help us honor you and seek justice in all our ways. Amen.

CHALLENGE:

In our politically charged society, may justice be established.

_____
_____
_____
_____
_____
_____
_____

A COOL SPIRIT

 **TODAY'S PASSAGE:**

Whoever restrains his words has knowledge, and he who has a cool spirit is a man of understanding. Even a fool who keeps silent is considered wise; when he closes his lips, he is deemed intelligent.

Proverbs 17:27-28

COMMENTARY:

From Garry: A wise person is careful in how they speak. They use restraint and self-control. My friend, G. Wright Doyle, in his book *Worship and Wisdom*, writes:

The person with real knowledge—the knowledge of God and His Word—will use words carefully. Rather than expressing his own opinion, he will ask what others think. If they are happy, he will share their joy. When they are sad, he will not rush in with advice, but will listen attentively and seek to understand, entering their world.

Proverbs teaches that the words of the wise are true and honest. There are also a few others. Proverbs 10:19 (ESV) says, "When words are many, transgression is not lacking, but whoever restrains his lips is prudent." A wise person's words are calm. Calm words from a cool spirit help one understand and allow for a good response rather than an emotional reaction.

Proverbs 15:1-2 (ESV) says, "A soft answer turns away wrath, but a harsh word stirs up anger. The tongue of the wise commends knowledge, but the mouths of fools pour out folly." A wise person speaks what is appropriate for the situation.

Proverbs 15:23 (ESV) says, "To make an apt answer is a joy to a man, and a word in season, how good it is!" G. Wright Doyle says this in his book, *Worship and Wisdom*:

> *If we know God, we shall seek to speak words that build others up according to the need of the occasion. The better we understand the mind of God, the less we shall engage in frivolous speech and ill-considered humor.*

From Ward: Communication is important for our community. Speaking the appropriate words in a situation can bring peace and success. Spoken words can evoke emotions and reflect them. Speaking positive words to another person will bring affirmation and hope. Speaking negative words to another can bring depression and disappointment. Many words we speak are for conversation and have no moral quality.

What subjects do we talk about the most? I encourage you to reflect on the subjects you frequently discuss at the end of this devotion. On the left side, write a column about what matters you anticipate you will talk about today. Then, at the end of the day, take this book and write on the right side what conversations you had today. These can be conversations with others as well as when you talk to yourself.

Are the two lists similar or different? Be honest. When talking about others and daily events, how often do you complain, gripe, or express frustration? Do you express hope, anticipation of success, satisfaction, or thankfulness? Did you encourage anyone today? Did anyone encourage you? How many conversations are only about your opinions and ideas? How much time do you spend listening to others and pondering their words? Finally, when thinking about the two lists, do any of your daily words need to change? Are you satisfied with the words you have spoken and the words you have heard?

These two proverbs remind us that sometimes, not responding in a conversation may be just as valuable as any words you could say. Wisdom can sometimes be displayed in what we do not say as well as what we do say. Words said in a heated conversation are rarely helpful. Keeping a cool spirit when speaking is a virtue. I must remember this, as I often say harsh words when I am angry. Then I am embarrassed and must apologize. I hope I am getting better at remaining quiet when I am emotionally upset. May all of us choose godly and helpful speech and refrain from bitter and harsh words.

From Frank C: I agree with your challenge—there is indeed great value in the self-control of our speech.

From Frank H.: Words have the power of life and death. Don't be reactive, but choose your words wisely.

From John: Through reading and studying the Bible, I believe that everything I do, say, or think originates from the heart. My brain will, in certain circumstances, want to take over and jump to some conclusion or cause me to say something I might not want to say. I have been told that it is better to think about what you are about to do, say, or think before you act on it. Essentially, listen to your heart, and you will act in a manner that honors the Lord. Keeping your mouth shut and listening helps you avoid being ridiculed for something you said but regretted later.

From Leslie: Very good word, Garry. I don't think I can add anything to this.

From Cindi: As I meditated on this, I was led to 2 Timothy 1:7 (RSV): "For God did not give us a spirit of timidity but a spirit of power and love and of self-control." I ask that the Lord make me bold in speaking of His love, but please keep me from speaking without restraint where I might offend.

From Wright: My words convict me! Just last night in our small group, I spoke far too much. I really need the Holy Spirit to come and give me self-control based on love for God and those around me. Thanks for this challenge, Garry.

From Doreen: Knowing when to speak and when to be silent is a gift of wisdom and often must be learned from experience. Some struggle with this. We must remember we aren't responsible for fixing others' problems by giving unsolicited advice. My listening skills have improved since beginning this study in Proverbs.

From Cynthia: When it bothers me how others speak, I need to look at myself and how I speak. We may speak out of turn when we feel that something is missing in our lives. I pray God erases all the words that left my mouth without His blessing.

PRAYER:

Lord, may I be careful in how I speak. Guard my lips, Lord. Amen.

CHALLENGE:

There is great value in self-control, especially in the matter of our speech.

_____
_____
_____
_____
_____
_____
_____

BE OPEN

🌳 TODAY'S PASSAGE:

Whoever isolates himself seeks his own desire; he breaks out against all sound judgment.

Proverbs 18:1

COMMENTARY:

From Garry: These translations provide more insight into today's passage:

- The Complete Jewish Bible says, "He who separates himself indulges his desires and shows contempt for sound advice of any kind," (Proverbs 18:1 [CJB]).
- The Free Bible Version says, "Selfish people only please themselves, they attack anything that makes good sense," (Proverbs 18:1 [FBV]).
- The Good News Translation states, "People who do not get along with others are interested only in themselves; they will disagree with what everyone knows is right," (Proverbs 18:1 [GNT]).

This proverb warns against being isolated and selfish, and ignoring the judgment of others. The wall of isolation is built out of pride and a refusal to listen to common sense. Building a wall around yourself out of your own stubborn pride cuts you off from the good advice others can give. It is unhealthy to shut others out.

From Ward: Despite all the means to connect with others via current technology, I think many folks feel isolated and alone. Our devices, like smartphones and social media, give us ways to communicate superficially. We can have a social friend and still not know the deepest hurts, desires, and needs they have. We all want intimate, deep relationships but still wonder how to form them. Part of this is shame, anxiety, fear of being rejected, and worrying that no one really cares about you.

This proverb reminds us that total isolation from others is not sound. I am an introvert and have a difficult time being in crowds and around people I do not know well. I want to withdraw from social functions, but I force myself to attend them because I know it is good for my soul.

- Harold S Kushner wrote, "None of us can be truly human in isolation."
- Robert Zemeckis has said, "We do not function well as human beings when we are in isolation." I sometimes forget that being with others can make me emotionally whole.
- S Kelley Harrell has written, "We do not heal in isolation, but in community."

Seeking a solution to my emotional hurt while being by myself generally does not bring complete resolution. We all need the input and support of our close friends. When God says in Genesis 2:18 (ESV), "It is not good that the man should be alone," He was not talking just about the first man, Adam. When the Christian church was formed, the book of Acts shows us that small groups appeared everywhere the Good News was preached. No one stayed a disciple of Jesus by being alone. Remember: community with believers provides an abundant life as Jesus' followers.

From Cynthia: I've found that you can learn a lot from a four-year-old. Children mirror what they see and hear and what they think is important. We get to know ourselves a little better through them. Generally, we learn more about ourselves by being around other people.

PRAYER:

Lord, may I not hold on to selfish pride that builds a wall. Help me value the community and what it offers. Amen.

CHALLENGE:

Be open to learn and to grow.

THE CLOSED-MINDED FOOL

TODAY'S PASSAGE:

> A fool takes no pleasure in understanding, but only in expressing his opinion.
> **Proverbs 18:2**

COMMENTARY:

From Garry: The previous verse spoke of a person who shows contempt for sound advice. A person like that is a fool. There seem to be quite a few proverbs about "the fool." I wonder why? Maybe the writer understood that one can learn from both negative and positive examples. The fool displays the behavior we ought to avoid.

- The Good News Translation says, "A fool does not care whether he understands a thing or not; all he wants to do is show how smart he is," (Proverbs 18:2 [GNT]).
- The Amplified Version states, "A [closed-minded] fool does not delight in understanding, But only in revealing his personal opinions [unwittingly displaying his self-indulgence and his stupidity]," (Proverbs 18:2 [AMP]).
- The Message Bible says, "Fools care nothing for thoughtful discourse; all they do is run off at the mouth," (Proverbs 18:2 [MSG]).

A fool is in love with their own ideas and enjoys spewing them out. They are the kind of person who would ask a question, not to learn, but to show everyone how clever they are.

From Ward: In a normal conversation, how much do you speak, and how much do you listen? I do not believe there is a proper ratio of talking to listening, but in a conversation, there should be some of each. Do you ever say a phrase like "I know it to be true that…?" And if you say those words, are you sure that the facts you state are correct? Today, we are overwhelmed with information from many sources but receive little wisdom. Many statements are written and proclaimed as facts when the words are opinions. Imaginations create stories that become myths and then become history. At the same time, the verification of the tale is as solid as the morning fog.

Too many of us want the world to exist exactly as we picture it in our minds, and our opinions reflect our perceptions. Understanding does not come from just talking to people who think like us but also from listening to our opponents. George Patton once said, "If everybody is thinking alike, then somebody isn't thinking."

News outlets today have stopped reporting events and instead evaluate and moralize events. This practice prevents the listener from forming their own opinion. When we do not have an accurate explanation of a circumstance, how can God speak to us? God's word to us is true, but many of our observations today are half-truths. God wants our eyes and ears to be open to what happens so that we can respond with kindness, goodness, compassion, and justice. When we close our eyes and ears to understanding, we block God's ability to bring his life into a situation.

Political, economic, and educational solutions do not establish God's kingdom on earth. Allowing God to speak and his spirit to move around us establishes righteousness and justice in the world. To achieve this goal, we need to have a correct understanding of our environment. Let us pray that the power of opinion that rules our news and speech may be broken and replaced by announcing truth to the world.

From John: One thing I truly enjoy is getting together with other pastors to discuss a specific topic or verses of scripture. I have learned that if I take my opinion to that meeting, it may be flawed. By accepting this, I have learned a great deal and gained valuable knowledge. If I close my mind to anything but my view, then I never learn or grow in knowledge but instead maintain my total ignorance.

From Frank: Garry, this is a good insight. And I appreciate you showing such a wide range of translations.

From Cindi: I can't help but remember Mr. T, who always said, "I pity the fool!" Ha!

From Doreen: This personality trait can destroy lives. It destroys not only the life of the person who speaks foolishly but also those around them.

From Cynthia: There are numerous scriptures that address this subject. It shocks me when someone isn't willing to listen to another viewpoint or get another opinion on important matters. Being busy also contributes to speaking without listening. In fact, I like this quote by Dallas Willard: "Hurry is the devil."

PRAYER:

Lord, may I not be like a fool who does not learn because he is stuck in his pride. Instead, may I be humble and open-minded in order to grow. Amen.

CHALLENGE:

Do not be like a senseless person who finds no pleasure in acquiring true wisdom. Watch out for careless displays of pride.

_____
_____
_____
_____
_____
_____
_____

CONCERN, NOT CONTEMPT

TODAY'S PASSAGE:

> *When wickedness comes, contempt comes also, and with dishonor comes disgrace.*
>
> **Proverbs 18:3**

COMMENTARY:

From Garry: What is wickedness? It is a total disregard for the fair and just and true. It is a rejection of that which is right and honorable. Wickedness and contempt go together.

What is contempt? It is the feeling that a person or a thing is beneath consideration. It is when people are humiliated and put down rather than encouraged and respected. It is when people are shamed rather than honored. How does it feel when you are shown no respect? It feels bad, doesn't it? What is it that causes worthlessness? It is wickedness.

- The Good News Translation says, "Sin and shame go together. Lose your honor, and you will get scorn in its place," (Proverbs 18:3 [GNT]).
- The Passion Translation says, "An ungodly man is always cloaked with disgrace, as dishonor and shame are his companions," (Proverbs 18:3 [TPT]).

From Ward: I have written before that I do not think I know any wicked people. I know people who have done wrong actions, but I never have thought of them as wicked or evil. Perhaps if I lived on another continent where the population was not familiar with the Ten Commandments, I might have a different experience. People exhibit evil behavior when they are completely self-centered and disregard the needs of others. I hope I have never treated anyone this way.

I think very little about honor. In Eastern cultures, honor is a crucial part of family status and community acceptance. This was likely true in the Middle East when this proverb was written. In that location, honor is inherited because of position, relationship, or character. In our Western culture, honor comes after achievement and performance.

In the Hebrew culture of the past, shame would come to a person who exhibited rogue behavior, as this did not reflect well on the family character. Conformity would bring honor to the group. The same is true for our relationship with God. When we act righteously, God is honored. When we say we are Christians and sin, then God receives no glory or honor. Our sinful acts affect more than ourselves and those we sin against. God wants to be known as a person of great value, and we can display His goodness through our godly acts. May we all refrain from those actions and words that bring disgrace and contempt to God and the community of believers.

From Frank: A strong challenge indeed!

From Doreen: Some perceive wickedness as a blatant act—some wicked actions are very apparent. But you can also be evil and subtle in *small* matters. This seems more commonplace to me, especially within the last few years. Some influential people *appear* to escape accountability for their actions in spite of disgracing those under them. We need to pray about how to respond to these situations.

From Cynthia: We need to start with our families to develop compassion for one another. We rarely view events the same way as others in life. We want to be understood, yet we are often blinded by our own desires and drive to be correct. It is not always easy to do the right thing or respond the right way. Forgiveness for others leaves a big space for God to come into your heart and gives you peace.

PRAYER:

Lord, help me honor people. Help me show respect. I do not want to live in shame and disgrace. Amen.

CHALLENGE:

> *Let no corrupting talk come out of your mouths, but only such as is good for building up, as fits the occasion, that it may give grace to those who hear. And do not grieve the Holy Spirit of God, by whom you were sealed for the day of redemption. Let all bitterness and wrath and anger and clamor and slander be put away from you, along with all malice. Be kind to one another, tenderhearted, forgiving one another, as God in Christ forgave you.*
> **Ephesians 4:29-32 (ESV)**

_____
_____
_____
_____
_____
_____
_____

DEEP AND REFRESHING

 **TODAY'S PASSAGE:**

The words of a man's mouth are deep waters; the fountain of wisdom is a bubbling brook.

Proverbs 18:4

COMMENTARY:

From Garry: This is a fascinating proverb. It can be interpreted in several ways. The two phrases can be seen as contrasting or complementing one another. Let me explain.

The first observation about the deep waters could mean that human nature is reluctant or unable to give itself away or that they are careful to only reveal part of their soul to others. The other interpretation is that the two phrases flow together as "synonymous parallelism." In this case, the second half of the proverb continues the idea presented in the first half. Wisdom is deep but also a continuous source of refreshing and beneficial ideas. Alfred, Lord Tennyson, in *In Memoriam*, wrote:

> *For words, like Nature, half reveal, And half conceal the Soul within.*

The Tyndale commentary suggests this proverb contrasts our human reluctance, or inability, to give ourselves away with the refreshing candor and clarity of true wisdom. When you consider the two parts of this proverb together, the Good News Translation becomes clear: "A person's words can be a source of wisdom, deep as the ocean, fresh as a flowing stream" (Proverbs 18:4 [GNT]). When I reflected on this proverb, I wrote in my journal: *Wisdom is deep down within your soul; let it flow so it can refresh the hearer.*

From Ward: What in nature represents life to you? At the end of this devotion, please write what images of nature display life to you. In the Hebrew culture, one metaphor is flowing water. A stream or moving water represents life. Wisdom should bring clarity to our souls and refreshment to our minds. God's truth is expressed in wisdom, and wisdom should bring life to us. In the same way, our words should bring life to ourselves and to others. How can we do this?

- Speaking words of encouragement, hope, comfort, and support
- Being more ready to listen than to criticize
- Allowing God to bring a solution for a struggle rather than believing we must have an answer to every trial
- In the same vein, not thinking we must create an instant answer to every predicament
- Trying to use each circumstance of life as an opportunity to refresh and renew our faith in God
- Remembering that God wants us to be wise, but that it may take a long time to reveal wisdom

God is never late, but he is rarely early. Lord, grant that we may drink from your bubbling brook of pure thinking each day.

From Cindi: Beautiful Proverb! I have been blessed to know many sisters in the faith who have helped me understand and apply scripture. As a young Mom, I was incredibly grateful for older members of our congregation who shared incredible insight with me. May we all be so blessed in the family of God!

From Doreen: We speak from our soul. You can learn a lot about someone by listening to them talk. The fountain of wisdom is like a deep underground spring, being released little by little. Through my study of the book of Proverbs, I have learned to pray for wisdom.

From Cynthia: John 7:38 (ESV) says, "Whoever believes in me, as the Scripture has said, 'Out of his heart will flow rivers of living water.'" Rivers represent nourishment and healing. If a river comes from me, I want it to be from God. *The source matters.*

PRAYER:

Father, give me the courage to be transparent with my close friends, and help me walk in the wisdom that refreshes and blesses. Amen.

CHALLENGE:

Open your soul and trust. Go to God, the Source of Wisdom.

_____
_____
_____
_____
_____
_____
_____

NOT GOOD

 **TODAY'S PASSAGE:**

It is not good to be partial to the wicked or to deprive the righteous of justice.
Proverbs 18:5

COMMENTARY:

From Garry: Note two additional versions of today's passage:

- The Contemporary English Version: "It's wrong to favor the guilty and keep the innocent from getting justice," (Proverbs 18:5 [CEV]).
- The Message Bible: "It's not right to go easy on the guilty, or come down hard on the innocent," (Proverbs 18:5 [MSG]).

The notes from the New English Translation highlight that the Hebrew term *Not Good* is a deliberate understatement intended to emphasize a worst-case scenario. It is, in fact, *Terrible*. It is terrible to show partiality and favor to the wicked by depriving the innocent of their rights. It is a perversion of justice.

In my journal, I wrote the term *Not Good* with an arrow on both sides. To the left side, I wrote *to honor the wicked*, and on the right side, I wrote *to be unfair to the innocent*. In other words, be completely fair.

To honor the wicked ← NOT GOOD → *To be unfair to the innocent*

From Ward: These last few devotions have been difficult to write because I do not believe there is only one correct way to view every situation. Life is mushy, and decisions can be tough. I am happy I am not a judicial authority.

How many good friends do you have? Please take a moment and write their names on the lines at the end of this devotion. How long have you known your best friends? Do these people consider you their best friend as well? Now, here is an interesting question. What if your good friend were to receive a negative consequence for a serious violation? Would you be willing to bend a rule, break a rule, or ignore a rule to prevent a negative conclusion? If so, then you are showing partiality. Is this wise? Should rules and regulations apply equally to our friends and to the people we do not know?

In Garry's comment, he writes, "Be completely fair." Does this apply to every struggle, every event, and every adventure we have? Romans 2:11 (ESV) says, "For God shows no partiality." If this is true for God, is this true for us also? In James 2:13b (NKJV), the author writes, "Mercy triumphs over judgment." Does this verse apply to the questions I have asked in this devotion? Please pause to ponder all these questions.

OK, I believe you have paused before reading this paragraph. I will give an answer. Maybe not the best one. The enforcement of laws can be lessened if the community and persons of authority agree. For example, in John 8, a lady is brought to Jesus. She has committed adultery, and the Biblical punishment was death. Jesus asks the crowd for anyone who has not sinned to start the execution. No one will execute the lady. So, the community surrounding Jesus and the lady agree that the death sentence is not an appropriate punishment for her situation. Mercy triumphs over judgment again.

As individuals, we must be careful not to override laws established by the community simply to make a friend happy. If an exemption or change in judgment is appropriate, we should ask for the community's help to bypass the judgment of a broken rule.

We should not show partiality toward the wicked. We should not punish the righteous. We must establish a community where the law is applied equally to all its members. Those in authority must not be harsh and vindictive to those who trespass. These are difficult tasks. May God grant all members of the community, both Christians and non-believers, not to be partial but also to show mercy where it is needed.

From Doreen: This verse can be paired with many others in Proverbs. The wicked will continue with their wicked ways until God intervenes. Some people act out in wicked ways because they have wounds from their past, and God may intervene with a good counselor. On the other hand, depriving the righteous of justice isn't fair or right. Judges need our prayers to discern what is just and decide whether it is more appropriate to punish or pardon.

PRAYER:

Lord, you value truth. Help me be completely fair in my dealings with both the guilty and the innocent. Amen.

CHALLENGE:

Change the "not good" to "good" by honoring justice.

_____
_____
_____
_____
_____
_____

A FOOL'S MOUTH

 **TODAY'S PASSAGE:**

A fool's lips walk into a fight, and his mouth invites a beating. A fool's mouth is his ruin, and his lips are a snare to his soul. The words of a whisperer are like delicious morsels; they go down into the inner parts of the body.

Proverbs 18:6-8

COMMENTARY:

From Garry: In this proverb, the Hebrew term used for *fool* is the most common one, and it is used fifty times in the book. It is amazing to me how often the behavior of the fool is described. This fool is dull and obstinate. He lacks concentration and thinks that wisdom can be just handed to him. He always thinks he is right. He likes his folly. He keeps going back to it.

The fundamental problem with the fool is that he rejects the fear of the Lord. As a result, he is a menace to society. Not only does he ruin the lives of those around him, but he also ruins his own life. His words create trouble for others and himself. He greedily gobbles up the morsels of gossip and spreads the lies that create misunderstanding and hurt feelings. Unfortunately, gossip does a lot of damage and affects how we view the person or the situation.

From Ward: Louis Nizer once wrote, "Some people will believe anything if you whisper it to them." Mark Twain wrote, "It is better to keep your mouth closed and let people think you are a fool than to open it and remove all doubt."

Our speech can be positive or negative, both through our words and our tone. What type of speech did Jesus use when he was on earth?

- He was not sarcastic.
- He never lied.
- He always stood for the truth and would not let it be ignored.
- Sometimes, he spoke with metaphors and parables.
- He invited his listeners to ponder.
- He did not insult others. When he calls Herod a fox in Luke 13:32, the Greek word is *jackal*, which Wikipedia describes as an opportunistic omnivore, predator, and scavenger. He is giving a description of how the king acts.
- He did not exaggerate or minimize the severity of an event.
- His focus was to use his words to proclaim God's word to us.
- He debated his detractors but without anger or bitterness.
- He respected the humble and attempted to open the eyes of the proud.
- He offered hope and kindness.
- He was not a showman, entertainer, dramatic actor, or comedian.
- He did not embarrass his opponents.
- When he spoke, he did not demand that his listeners agree with him.

All these descriptions are the opposite of being a foolish speaker. Hopefully, we will follow Jesus' example in our speech.

From Cindi: I know firsthand that hurtful slander and gossip can be devastating. I strive with God's help not to be hurtful when speaking of others. Psalm 19:14a (RSV) says, "Let the words of my mouth and the meditation of my heart be acceptable in thy sight, O LORD!"

From Doreen: A person like the one in this proverb has an empty place in their soul. Their words and actions have a negative impact on their life and the people around them. I know people who are like this and often pray for them and their families. Ultimately, only God can fill their soul and bring healing. Hopefully, they will then see the error of their ways and make changes to live a better, more peaceful life.

From Cynthia: It's embarrassing when you must set boundaries or when boundaries must be set for you because of what comes out of your mouth. Relationships and businesses are ruined because of these misunderstandings. The church has been harmed by believers speculating and spreading idle gossip. I ask for forgiveness when I am foolish with my words. I pray for ministers and their families because they are targeted by the enemy. We need to be lifting people up with our words.

PRAYER:

Lord, help me take these warnings about a fool seriously and use my mouth to bless others with truth and grace. Amen.

CHALLENGE:

Don't let foolish behavior or talk destroy you.

_____
_____
_____
_____
_____
_____
_____

A SLUGGARD'S WAYS

 **TODAY'S PASSAGE:**

Whoever is slack in his work is a brother to him who destroys.
                                                                Proverbs 18:9

COMMENTARY:

From Garry: My father told me many times, "If you are going to do a task, do it right." This proverb reveals a characteristic of the sluggard. When you look at the sluggard in Proverbs, you discover several characteristics.

First, you discover a person who will not begin things. Proverbs 6:9-11 (ESV) says, "How long will you lie there, O sluggard? When will you arise from your sleep? A little sleep, a little slumber, a little folding of the hands to rest, and poverty will come upon you like a robber and want like an armed man."

Second, a sluggard will not finish things. Proverbs 19:24 (ESV) says, "The sluggard buries his hand in the dish and will not even bring it back to his mouth."

Third, you also discover that the sluggard will not face issues. He believes his own excuses because he rationalizes his own laziness. Proverbs 22:13 (ESV) states, "The sluggard says, 'There is a lion outside! I shall be killed in the streets!'"

Fourth, the sluggard is restless. Proverbs 21:25-26 (ESV) says, "The desire of the sluggard kills him, for his hands refuse to labor. All day long, he craves and craves, but the righteous gives and does not hold back." Proverbs 13:4 (ESV) also says, "The soul of the sluggard craves and gets nothing, while the soul of the diligent is richly supplied."

From Ward: For many Christian scholars, laziness is considered a sin. Sometimes, Bible translations call this action slothful. Colossians 3:23 (ESV) speaks to servants, saying, "Whatever you do, work heartily, as for the Lord and not for men." No one is born lazy. It is a learned behavior that can be changed.

The causes of laziness are varied. There can be a physical reason, like lack of sleep, poor nutrition, or exhaustion. The person may be fearful, hopeless, have no interest in the work, or believe they cannot complete the task. The worker may be taking a rest or a break. Additionally, one person may work more slowly or deliberately, while another person may view this as laziness.

We must be careful not to judge or reject another person because of his work speed or emotional health. Those who are supervisors and co-workers of someone who is being viewed as slothful can provide an environment for the less focused worker to succeed. These actions include:

- Having a reasonable goal for each task
- Showing each worker the ultimate purpose of their work—letting the worker know the task is not mindless or repetitive, but has a meaningful objective
- Breaking larger tasks into small ones and accomplishing those first
- Checking to see that the worker's physical health is good
- Giving encouragement, compassion, and kindness, and reminding the worker that success is possible

Let us not give up on those who work slower than we do. But offer help that allows others to take joy in their work and not shrink back from completing a task.

From Doreen: While some modern conveniences have made it easier to be lazy, the choice is ultimately an individual one. I appreciate the conveniences that make my world easier. But, at times, I revert to the "old-fashioned way" of doing things, primarily to keep myself more physically active.

From Frank: This is good, as always, Garry. What about a tougher challenge, like "be diligent in your work" or "work as if you are working for the Lord "?

From Cynthia: Children are taught early in life to be lazy or disciplined. People can learn to develop good habits, but it is often more difficult the older they get. Many books address the subject of goal setting and habit tracking. Motivators and coaches work to right the scales of productivity. Then, some people are too busy to develop healthy habits or routines—too busy for family and too busy for God.

When I was 14 years old, I wrote Scripture in big letters on my wall. My mother wasn't impressed with my efforts and wouldn't let me paint my wise mural. Alas, declaring my intentions to be disciplined was about as faint as the mural on my wall.

PRAYER:

Father, help me do things right and not be lazy in my work. Amen.

CHALLENGE:

Laziness is not good.

_____
_____
_____
_____
_____
_____
_____

WHERE IS YOUR TRUST?

 **TODAY'S PASSAGE:**

The name of the LORD is a strong tower; the righteous man runs into it and is safe. A rich man's wealth is his strong city, and like a high wall in his imagination.

Proverbs 18:10-11

COMMENTARY:

From Garry: These two proverbs contrast places of safety. One is a strong tower offering security and protection. The other is a strong city, with high walls offering safety in the imagination of the wealthy person. One is trustworthy, the other is not. One is based on the character of God and is spiritual in nature. The other is based on the temporary limitations of the material. Note these two versions of this proverb:

- The Good News Translation says, "The LORD is like a strong tower, where the righteous can go and be safe. Rich people, however, imagine that their wealth protects them like high, strong walls around a city," (Proverbs 18:10-11 [GNT]).
- The Message Bible says, "GOD's name is a place of protection—good people can run there and be safe. The rich think their wealth protects them; they imagine themselves safe behind it," (Proverbs 18:10-11 [MSG]).

The Masoretic text of these verses suggests that security is the primary focus here. In other words, are you going to trust God or money? One observation is that these two verses, coupled together, are a loud criticism of this misguided faith. The use of the term *imagination* shows that one's wealth alone is a futile place of refuge. Paul wrote Timothy these words of advice:

> *As for the rich in this present age, charge them not to be haughty, nor to set their hopes on the uncertainty of riches, but on God, who richly provides us with everything to enjoy. They are to do good, to be rich in good works, to be generous and ready to share, thus storing up treasure for themselves as a good foundation for the future, so that they may take hold of that which is truly life.*
> **1 Timothy 6:17-19 (ESV)**

From Ward: This is a different perspective on these verses. The words *protect* and *protection* do not appear in the original Hebrew (Old Testament) or the original Greek (New Testament) in our Bible. Yet these two words are used frequently in today's sermons and written articles. If you doubt me, please look at resource books that were published before 1968. They include books such as the *King James Version of the Bible, Vines Complete Expository Dictionary,* or *Young's Analytical Concordance.* In contemporary publications dating back to 1980, such as *The Living Bible* and the *NIV*, the reader will find "protection" in a word search.

In our modern era, many Christians in the West deeply believe God will protect us from all harm, injury, and sickness. So, Western translators will add these words to their English translations. The authors are taking the Hebrew and Greek words for *keep, watch over, guard, and tend* and translating these words into the English word *protect*. This is not wise. We must read the Bible as it is written and not change the meaning to want what we want it to say. We must fit our theology to follow God's word and not change God's word to fit our established conclusions.

Protect states that no harm will happen. God never promises us this. The ancients did not assume "God promises to keep us from all harm," but "what do we do when danger, famine, disease, or invasion come?" The following verses, 2 Timothy 2:3, 3:12, 4:5, I Peter 4:12, 5:9, and Romans 12:12, remind us that suffering, pain, and persecution will come to Christian believers. Freedom from pain, want, illness, and distress is a gift from God that comes to some, but not to all. A strong tower is available from God, but it is not a 100 percent assurance of no harm or injury. Dr. Jim Fleming has stated that there is no 100 percent successful defense. There is always a bigger arrow, rock, warrior, or army that can defeat anyone. Our response is to trust God for comfort and rescue, not for freedom from inconvenience, waiting, loss, or pain.

There is a sad but increasing negative consequence of the rising focus in current Christianity that God is pledged to always keep us away from any harmful events. I have friends who have left the faith and become non-believers because some terrible suffering happened, and God did not prevent this. They rejected any belief in God because intense suffering happened to a godly person. Proclaiming the narrative that God blocks harm and suffering is not correct and not an evangelistic testimony. We must be honest in our description of God's character. We cannot tell others that being a Christian involves no early death of loved ones, no physical handicaps, no wars, and no starvation. Outside the US, there are still millions of Christians who are poor and have little access to health care. These brothers and sisters are overwhelmed with suffering while still maintaining their faith. Are Christians in the US able to do the same?

My trust is in what the Bible *really* says. I trust what God has told us in the past. Psalm 34:19 (NKJV) states, "Many *are* the afflictions of the righteous, But the LORD delivers him out of them all." There is deliverance, but not prevention from afflictions.

Let us not be deluded by contemporary Christian writers and speakers. They insist that the lack of adverse events for citizens of the US is the standard for God's people everywhere and throughout all centuries. This conclusion is not true. Trust in the Lord. Trust in what the Bible really says. Do not trust in those who do not know the history of God's dealings with his people. Take time to read older translations of the Bible. The chapters may not be as easy to read as the current ones. Still, the translations are more accurate about suffering, pain, and rescue.

May God speak clearly to us as we read His Word and cause us to follow his path faithfully each day.

From Leslie: Good thoughts.

From John: I believe this scripture gets to the heart of who our God is; the One who can grant us freedom and salvation, or the one who traps us with lies and statements about how "everyone is doing it." I believe all of us who have found salvation have been, at one time or another, chasing the lie. When we were chasing Satan's lie, we had moments of happiness. But once we learned we were on the wrong track and turned to the Lord, we picked up our cross and followed Jesus. And we found the Truth, and unending JOY!

From Doreen: Recent years have proven that God is a much stronger tower than our savings or investment accounts are. Trusting in God is a better fortress in which to live. My husband has been retired for several years. Recently, I quit my job—a job that was to help fund our adventures. I quit to prove to myself that God is taking care of us and that we can survive without my part-time paycheck. The Lord is providing as He always does.

From Cynthia: One thing I love is hearing about humble, wealthy people whose purpose is to help others by giving freely. They haven't forgotten about their origins. We must set our minds on Christ and stop thinking about wealth to the exclusion of others. The world was created by God. He created an abundance of wonderful possessions to share with everyone. Things aren't meant to last forever. We can take Jesus everywhere we go. He's our Friend and Brother. Jesus didn't bequeath furniture, jewelry, or property. He gave us His precious heart.

PRAYER:

Lord, You alone are my strong tower. May I trust in You above my material wealth. Amen.

CHALLENGE:

> *But I will sing of your strength; I will sing aloud of your steadfast love in the morning. For you have been to me a fortress and a refuge in the day of my*

distress. O my Strength, I will sing praises to you, for you, O God, are my fortress, the God who shows me steadfast love.

Psalm 59:16-17 (ESV)

HAUGHTY OR HUMBLE?

 **TODAY'S PASSAGE:**

Before destruction a man's heart is haughty, but humility comes before honor.
Proverbs 18:12

COMMENTARY:

From Garry: Proverbs 16:18 (ESV) is similar: "Pride goes before destruction, and a haughty spirit before a fall." The very first step towards wisdom is the fear of the Lord. A heart that is haughty opposes this step. A heart that is proud and self-centered only sees itself and is blind to those around him.

Proverbs 15:33 (ESV) says, "The fear of the LORD is instruction in wisdom, and humility comes before honor." Jesus taught the way of service above self. Mark 10:42-45 explains it well:

And Jesus called them to him and said to them, "You know that those who are considered rulers of the Gentiles lord it over them, and their great ones exercise authority over them. But it shall not be so among you. But whoever would be great among you must be your servant, and whoever would be first among you must be slave of all. For even the Son of Man came not to be served but to serve, and to give his life as a ransom for many."
Mark 10:42-25 (ESV)

And Micah 6:8 (ESV) says, "He has told you, O man, what is good; and what does the LORD require of you but to do justice, and to love kindness, and to walk humbly with your God?"

From Ward: Being humble means you want to honor God. And God will honor you, if you are humble. The haughty and arrogant pursue only their own goals and feast only on their own success. What have others said about these two attributes?

- John Ruskin has written, "I believe the first test of a truly great man is in his humility."
- Andy Stanley has said, "Knowledge alone makes Christians haughty. Application makes us holy."
- An anonymous quote is, "More people would learn from their mistakes, if they weren't so busy denying them."
- Leo Tolstoy wrote, "Christianity with its doctrines of humility, forgiveness and love is incompatible with the state (the government) with its haughtiness, violence, punishment and wars."
- Friedrich Nietzsche wrote, "The higher we soar, the smaller we appear to those who cannot fly."
- Another unnamed quote is "Arrogance is a roadblock on the highway to wisdom."
- Jean Vanier wrote, "Growth begins when we begin to accept our own weakness."

These are great thoughts about the value of humility and the worthlessness of arrogance and conceit. Let us remember the proud consider themselves better than they are. This leads to eventual failure, while the modest will receive a good report from the community.

From Frank: I think humility is the key to our life—following Jesus, who came to serve.

From Cindi: In talking with people who are living outside of the church, I often hear how Christians are judgmental and like to show how religious they are. But I rarely hear them saying how much like a servant they are. I pray, dear Lord, that you will reveal whatever is prideful and haughty in me. Replace it with an attitude of servitude and grace and let me always give You the glory.

From Cynthia: Pride seems to be a quick fix to feeling good about oneself. The people I admire most have a servant's heart. They are humble. In college, there was a young woman (Elizabeth) who bowed her head and quietly prayed, especially when groups were rowdy. During those moments, I wondered how effective her prayers would be. As with this woman, being humble takes restraint, discipline, and thought.

From Doreen: Sometimes it's hard not to let pride impede what we're asked to do. I do my best not to look down on others. I may not like someone or approve of what they're doing or the way they're living. However, it's not my place to judge them. I try to remember where I came from in my faith walk and in my life.

PRAYER:

Father, may I walk humbly before You today. Fill my heart with a humble spirit because I want to be like You, Lord. Amen.

CHALLENGE:

Is pride blocking your way?

_____
_____
_____
_____
_____
_____
_____

LISTEN, LISTEN

 **TODAY'S PASSAGE:**

> *If one gives an answer before he hears, it is his folly and shame.*
>
> Proverbs 18:13

COMMENTARY:

From Garry: Jumping ahead of a conversation and speaking before listening is rude. It reveals that the person has a low regard for what the other is saying. It might show that the person is so absorbed in his own ideas, he rushes to display his own opinion.

Proverbs 18:2 (ESV) states, "A fool takes no pleasure in understanding, but only in expressing his opinion."

Proverbs 18:17 (ESV) says, "The one who states his case first seems right, until the other comes and examines him." This proverb is a picture of poor listening. I have been guilty of that. Sometimes I am not careful because I am so intent on being heard.

The Passion Translation says, "Listen before you speak, for to speak before you've heard the facts will bring humiliation," (Proverbs 18:13 [TPT]).

From Ward: For today's comment, I thought I would ask the web browser Google what good results come from listening. Google wrote:

- Understanding others' perspectives.
- Building trust.
- Resolving conflicts.
- Improving relationships.
- Enhancing productivity.
- Fostering empathy.
- Gaining knowledge.

- Showing respect.
- Avoiding misunderstandings.
- Making better decisions.

I guess Google has some wisdom to offer. There are benefits to being a good listener. Do you ever see these gains from listening to others? I encourage you to think about whether you are a thoughtful listener and if you have any need to be a better one. Doug Larson once wrote:

> *Wisdom is the reward you get for a lifetime of listening when you'd have preferred to talk.*
>
> **Doug Larson**

From Cindi: Lord, give me the humble attitude that reminds me to really listen and to put other's interests above my own.

From Cynthia: The closer we get to trusting Jesus, the less attention we need on us and the less we feel the need to offer our opinions and thoughts. We can't be taken seriously when talking out of turn.

I'm surprised when people ask me for advice because I used to give advice freely, even when the other party did not request it. Spoiler alert: No one appreciates unsolicited advice! If someone is talking too much, ask them if they are anxious about that topic. Ask if you can be of any help. They probably won't expect that reaction.

From Doreen: I struggled with this when I was younger. Being around someone who constantly interrupts showed me how annoying it can be to others, so I have worked to change this habit. Learning to listen and respond afterward is a much more helpful response. You might even change your response if you wait to hear the entire story.

PRAYER:

Father, help me be a good listener. You have created me with two ears and one mouth. Help me be slow to speak and quick to listen. Amen.

CHALLENGE:

Often, we are quick to speak and slow to listen. It should be the other way around.

_____
_____
_____
_____
_____
_____
_____

THE DARKNESS OF DEPRESSION

 **TODAY'S PASSAGE:**

A man's spirit will endure sickness, but a crushed spirit who can bear?
Proverbs 18:14

COMMENTARY:

From Garry: When a person is sick, they can possibly endure the pain. The spiritual state can supersede physical illness. The Message Bible says, "A healthy spirit conquers adversity, but what can you do when the spirit is crushed" (Proverbs 18:14 [MSG])? Depression is like being smashed or crushed. The darkness of depression breaks the will so that there is a loss of vitality, nothing but despair, and emotional pain. The Passion Translation says, "The will to live sustains you when you're sick, but depression crushes courage and leaves you unable to cope" (Proverbs 18:14 [TPT]).

What is one to do when depression creates darkness all around? When we reach a point of despair, we can lift our heads to the One who shines the light.

- In John 8:12b (ESV), Jesus said, "I am the light of the world. Whoever follows me will not walk in darkness, but have the light of life." God can bring light to the darkness!
- 1 Thessalonians 5:23-24 (ESV) says, "Now may the God of peace himself sanctify you completely, and may your whole spirit and soul and body be kept blameless at the coming of our Lord Jesus Christ. He who calls you is faithful; he will surely do it."
- I love the benediction in 2 Thessalonians 3:16 (ESV), "Now may the Lord of peace himself give you peace at all times in every way. The Lord be with you all."

From Ward: I have clinical depression. This means depression is caused by chemical imbalances in my brain, not by a tragic event. All of us can experience depression, sadness, grief, and turmoil. It is a normal part of life. Some of my sadness came from setting plans for my life and not talking to God first. I was not listening to God.

I failed to share my hurts with competent, mature believers. Their insights and listening ears would have made my struggles easier to bear. But I did not know how to reach out.

My viewpoint of life was incorrect. I saw each struggle as a stumbling stone, a wall too high to climb, a dead-end road. I did not realize that God was walking beside me. He could bring me to others who had experienced the same struggles, and I could ask for prayers, comfort, and encouragement.

I have learned that I must take time to relax and try to find ways to enjoy life rather than trying to solve all my anxieties on my own. Additionally, I have learned:

- Eat a proper diet.
- Get regular exercise. Even 10 minutes a day helps, especially if you can get outdoors.
- Have varied activities and friends—close friends who will listen carefully to your pain and not offer light advice. Ask a trusted friend to tell you if they see anything that might need to change in your life to help with the depression. This is very difficult to do.
- Get a proper amount of sleep. Too much or too little makes it more difficult to fight depression.
- Make regular plans or schedules for the day or week and actually do them. To slough off regular activities like walking, doing the laundry, and paying bills can add to a sense of "I am lost."
- Keep a regular quiet time—speaking to God and listening for Him to speak. Add praise and thanksgiving to every prayer you have.
- Do not expect the future or more money to totally solve your depression. We cannot buy our way out of depression.

Extreme depression will pass in time, but it will probably return at some point. We must face depression directly and be willing to use prayer, medicine, and professional counseling. Do not ignore depression or underestimate its power to overwhelm you and deceive you. Depression can change your way of thinking and your ability to handle everyday activities. We can deceive ourselves and view a situation incorrectly.

Depression enhances this deception. It can make us too introspective and too subjective about our needs and our solutions. May all those facing depression know there are solutions for help and reach out to find them.

From Wright: This is a good message, Garry. I mean, they are all good, but this is especially good because you start by acknowledging the reality of depression. Then you move to the Lord and to His Word.

From Frank C.: I love knowing Jesus is the Light of the World in times of darkness.

From Leslie: I love your prayer. Good word, Garry.

From Cindi: I am so grateful to have God's Word and His promises to lean on when the darkness of the world is overbearing. My favorite is "Surely goodness and mercy shall follow me all the days of my life" Psalm 23:6 (RSV).

From Frank H.: Depression can create a darkness so intense that one might believe that light cannot penetrate it. But Jesus is the Light of the world, and His Light can penetrate the darkest night, heart, or mind. The dawn is coming, and His name is Jesus.

From Cynthia: Today's passage is a warning for us to be gentle with each other. We don't know the trouble others are facing, and we aren't to judge. The world tells us to dominate, compete, and compare ourselves to each other. But we have the power and responsibility to uplift each other with encouragement. We have many opportunities to listen to hurting people.

From Doreen: Depression is a hard thing. I've experienced it in my life. In my research, I learned that a poor diet can have an impact on our mental well-being because of nutrient deficiencies. I also learned that exercise is one of the best remedies for anxiety and depression. The release of endorphins and feel-good hormones makes good changes in our bodies.

Of course, turning to God helps tremendously as well. We must learn to stop overthinking and give our concerns to God. We must stop listening to lies that we hear in our mind. Now, when I get angry, anxious, or depressed, I pray, exercise, and think about what I've been eating. I also tell evil to leave me in the Name of Jesus. I tell myself to stop thinking the thoughts that I'm thinking and realize that God is in control, not me. It's amazing how much my emotions have changed in the last decade or so since studying this topic.

PRAYER:

Lord, You have told us to cast all our cares on You because You care for us. Thank You that Your mercies are new every morning. Great is Your faithfulness. Amen.

CHALLENGE:

No matter what you are going through, God is more than ready to help you through it.

_____
_____
_____
_____
_____
_____
_____

A DISCERNING HEART

 **TODAY'S PASSAGE:**

> *An intelligent heart acquires knowledge, and the ear of the wise seeks knowledge.*
>
> **Proverbs 18:15**

COMMENTARY:

From Garry: Note the following translations:

- The Message Bible says, "Wise men and women are always learning, always listening for fresh insights," (Proverbs 18:15 [MSG]).
- The Complete Jewish Bible says it this way: "The mind of a person with discernment gets knowledge, and the ear of the wise seeks knowledge," (Proverbs 18:15 [CJB]).
- The Passion Translation states, "The spiritually hungry are always ready to learn more, for their hearts are eager to discover new truths," (Proverbs 18:15 [TPT]).

By listening carefully to what you hear and discerning what is heard to grow and acquire knowledge, you develop wisdom. Wisdom is more than knowledge; it is how you live.

As I spend time thinking about this verse, questions come to my mind: What is my motivation when I encounter knowledge? What do I seek? How do I adequately "discern" a matter before me? As I thought about these questions, my mind turned to Hebrews 5:14 (ESV): "But solid food is for the mature, for those who have their powers of discernment trained by constant practice to distinguish good from evil." The lifestyle of a person affects how they listen and acquire knowledge. A holy life enables greater discernment. The more we practice right living, the more we can discern that which is truly good.

From Ward: No one needs a college education to become wise. We do not need a degree, a certificate, or a license to obtain wisdom. There is no study course, no specific school, and no training manual to develop shrewdness in our minds. We can read wise words written by others. We can listen to the wisdom said by others. We can develop wisdom by reflecting on our experiences. But if wisdom does not become a part of our daily thoughts, then whatever we have read or heard is just the same as advertising slogans.

Few people find wisdom written on T-shirts. Wisdom becomes part of us as we have insightful friends and family members who can reinforce those precepts. Someone once wrote, "Knowledge is power." Perhaps that is true for some, but knowledge not put into action is emptiness, a wasted education. God's truths revealed to us are the instructions for how we should live. The best ongoing knowledge for us to possess is an understanding of how God wants us to live in a broken and sometimes cruel world.

No one can become truly wise by living alone. Cartoons that show a guru perched atop a mountain dispensing adages to all who approach is a false image of obtaining understanding. We become wise as we spend time with others, handling struggles, solving disputes, and comforting those in sorrow. The people most in touch, most aware, and most sympathetic with others are the wisest. As I wrote above, this does not require completing a class. May God grant us knowledge of His will and ways so that we might be loving supporters to those we know and meet.

From Cindi: Learning and studying, especially scripture and history, have always been a joy to me. It started as just learning to become more informed. So, I could know more! Now, I am at a place where I begin my studies, asking God to speak to me and reveal His truth in what I am learning, so that I may know Him more. It has made my journey more exciting and my reliance on God stronger.

From Cynthia: Gone are the days when we sat on the lawn sipping tea with friends or family. (The glare from natural light would impair reading on our devices.) I feel like family was a more central part of our lives a century ago.

Simplify your life. Don't waste the years struggling for something that is unimportant. Don't burden yourself with possessions. Keep your needs and wants simple, and enjoy what you have. Don't destroy your peace of mind by looking back and worrying about the past. Live in the present. Simplify!

From Doreen: This verse changed my life. To me, it means never stop learning. We can even gain wisdom from bad situations and experiences.

PRAYER:

Lord, give me an open mind that is eager to learn fresh new insights to love You with all my mind and heart. And help me do Your holy will as I grow in knowledge. Amen.

CHALLENGE:

What do you seek? Why?

_____
_____
_____
_____
_____
_____
_____

GIFT GIVING

🌳 TODAY'S PASSAGE:

A man's gift makes room for him and brings him before the great.

Proverbs 18:16

COMMENTARY:

From Garry: In this proverb, the Hebrew word for *gift* is *mattan*. This word is more neutral than the other Hebrew term for *gift* (*sohad*), which is translated as a "bribe." Proverbs 17:8 (ESV) says, "A bribe is like a magic stone in the eyes of the one who gives it; wherever he turns, he prospers." Proverbs 17:23 (ESV) says, "The wicked accepts a bribe in secret to pervert the ways of justice."

While bribes are wrong, gift-giving is not only innocent, but the courtesy of giving is also a blessing. My wife loves giving gifts! Especially this time of year, she really enjoys the season of expressing love through gifts. "Love came down at Christmas, love all lovely, love divine" (Rossetti, "Love Came Down at Christmas," verse one).

From Ward: Giving is an essential part of being a Christian. Whom do you like to give gifts to? Who likes to give gifts to you? Please take a moment and write on the lines at the end of the devotion and list the gifts you like to give. Are these all physical items? Did you list actions like smiles, hugs, a kind word, or a text? Giving can encompass many styles and offers. There are many positive reasons to give: celebration, thankfulness, friendship, reconciliation, assistance, and comfort. There are some negative reasons, too, such as buying a friendship or influencing and manipulating another person.

Our generosity gives us a good reputation, even among those who do not know God. St Francis reminds us that in giving, we receive. As we are generous to others, God will be generous to us. Not at the same time, not in the same amount, and not in the same way, but God will reward our generosity.

God freely gives life to all people, whether or not we acknowledge Him. Many of God's gifts require no response from us, such as rain, air, or plants that grow. How many gifts do we present to others where we remain content if no thank you is offered? Let us not treat God the same way. Let us remember this as we set aside time regularly to thank God for the overwhelming gifts He provides for us each day.

From Doreen: When I first read this, I immediately thought of a man's gift being the skill or talent that God gave him. Someone with great skill or talent (his gift) could be sought by the rich and famous.

From John: One of the most important things my late wife taught me was how important it was to help others, and we did that by giving them gifts. Those gifts were unsolicited and were given as often as possible anonymously. It was always great to be present, if possible, when that individual received their gift. In a lot of instances, the gift was something in the form of service or physical help to an individual. It always amazed me to hear the phrase, "You didn't have to do that." I learned through my late wife to cherish that statement.

From Cynthia: Sincere givers are easily identifiable; it's easy to spot insincere givers as well. God blesses people who worship Him and develop a giving spirit. Our God gives generously of *His* time and resources—we can never out-give our God.

PRAYER:

Lord, thank You for giving us the greatest gift of all! Thank You for loving the world so much You took the form of a tiny, helpless baby and lived among us. You offer the gift of grace, forgiveness, and eternal life to all who open Your gift by faith. Amen.

CHALLENGE:

Be like Christ and be a giving person!

THE TRUTH IS THE ISSUE

TODAY'S PASSAGE:

The one who states his case first seems right, until the other comes and examines him.

Proverbs 18:17

COMMENTARY:

From Garry: A legal case has many components for a reason. Legal disputes are settled after cross-examination. There are at least two sides to the story, and sometimes more. Careful, diligent searching is necessary to get to the truth. The aim in court cases is to get to the truth, and then for the jury to look at all the angles to come to a fair verdict.

The Message Bible says, "The first speech in a court case is always convincing—until the cross-examination starts," (Proverbs 18:17 [MSG])!

The New Century Version states, "The person who tells one side of a story seems right, until someone else comes and asks questions," (Proverbs 18:17 [NCV]).

From Ward: Have you ever served on a jury or been involved in a civil court case? If so, you realize there are often more than two sides to every dispute. I have served on three juries. For two of them, resolving the case was clear. For the third one, the decision of the suit took a little time to decide. Because we live in a sinful world, truth-telling is not always at the forefront of everyone's mind. Deciding what is true and what is false is not easy.

In James 5:12b (NKJV), it is written, "Do not swear…with any other oath. But let your 'Yes' be 'Yes' and *your* 'No,' 'No,' lest you fall into judgment." Our speech should be pure and trustworthy so that no one would suspect that we are telling a lie. There should be no reason to take an oath when we proclaim we are telling the truth. To take an oath means that sometimes we are lying, and sometimes we are speaking the truth. We should be known by those in the church and those in the community as faithful in our speech to relate events correctly. God's word and purpose to us are always true, and our declarations to the world should be, too. When our testimony of situations is truthful, we display our faithful relationship with God. And that is what I want the world to notice.

From Kyle: The following explanation regarding Proverbs 18:17 is found on the website *Let God Be True* (https://letgodbetrue.com/proverbs/index/chapter-18/proverbs-18-17/):

> Any man can sound reasonable when he speaks first and personally presses for his own cause. The absence of contrary facts or counter opinions, and his emotional and fervent appeals, can give credence to most any claim. Anything sounds good in a vacuum. But, all propositions must be tried by opposing arguments to prove their validity. The learned apostle Paul wisely wrote, "Prove all things; hold fast that which is good"(1 Thessalonians 5:21 [KJV]).
>
> Wise men prove all things. The Jews and the Romans allowed the accused to defend himself before judgment was passed. The Law of Moses required diligent examinations in all matters of hearsay, and it would not accept the testimony or witness of one man in any matter. One of the great prerogatives of kings, or any person in authority, is to make such inquisitions.
>
> Solomon wrote this to teach wise discretion when judging accusations, declarations, and propositions. This is wisdom—the power of right judgment! Truth can withstand intense examination, but most causes are not truthful. Challenging unsubstantiated claims will often expose them as false and frivolous. "The simple believeth every word: but the prudent man looketh well to his going" (Proverbs 14:15 [KJV]).

From Cynthia: God is my ultimate Judge, for which I'm grateful. When we make snap judgments because we don't question what we see and hear, God is good regardless.

From Doreen: There are always two sides to every story. It's easy to listen to one side, especially if you're listening to a friend.

From Leslie: There is an old Eagles song by Don Henley that has this line: "There's three sides to every story, baby, There's yours, and there's mine, and the cold hard truth" (from "Long Way Home"). Lord, help us be objective and see others' viewpoints.

PRAYER:

Lord, thank You for the legal system whose goal is truth and justice. Amen.

CHALLENGE:

Let all concerned speak to get to the truth of the matter.

_____
_____
_____
_____
_____
_____
_____

A COIN TOSS

TODAY'S PASSAGE:

The lot puts an end to quarrels and decides between powerful contenders.

Proverbs 18:18

COMMENTARY:

From Garry: Sometimes, when two parties come to a disagreement and there is no compromise, a lot can be cast, a coin toss can be used, or a drawing of straws can ease the tension. It is something neutral that can prevent fighting. The casting of lots was an ancient practice in Israel that sought God's leading. When interests and opinions clashed, a lot would be cast to determine God's guidance in a difficult matter. Providence played a determining role in the casting of lots.

The Message Bible says, "You may have to draw straws when faced with a tough decision," (Proverbs 18:18 [MSG]). The Common English Bible states, "The dice settle conflicts and keep strong opponents apart," (Proverbs 18:18 [CEB]). There were times in the Bible when the casting of a lot would reveal the truth about a matter and expose the guilty party.

From Ward: Gambling is not something I do. Neither do I like games of chance. So, I do not buy lottery tickets, play poker, or go to casinos. I will let others do that. To me, those choices are just ways to lose your money quickly and have no fun while becoming poorer. To the ancients, throwing lots and divination of dead animals seemed a reasonable way to make decisions. When a community does not know the laws of physics, chemistry, and biology, life appears to be random, unpredictable, and unstable. God understood this, so in His word, the Bible, He repeatedly tells us to trust Him and to know His rules.

The New International Version (NIV) of the Bible uses the word "trust" with the word "God" 42 times. The word "know" with "God" appears 249 times. God wants us to trust in Him and not in dice, sticks, or dead animal organs. God wants us to know His rules and follow His ways rather than following the words of a person in a trance. God knows that much of life consists of unexpected events and surprising losses. We should not be afraid or worried but believe God will comfort us and help us recover from any tragic situation.

From Cynthia: Making decisions is difficult for many people. I see where powerful contenders would need a neutral solution to move forward. Right or wrong, powerful contenders have opinions. This prayer is just right for trusting in God's providence, which promotes wise choices.

From Cindi: Like Momma said, "Life isn't always fair!" Things don't have to go our way all the time. Sometimes, just accepting the outcome is the most peaceful path.

From Doreen: It is amazing how long this practice has been used.

PRAYER:

Lord, help me trust You and look to Your guidance in matters that need to be resolved. Amen.

CHALLENGE:

You can trust God's providence.

_____
_____
_____
_____
_____
_____

GUARDING GOOD RELATIONSHIPS

🌳 TODAY'S PASSAGE:

> *A brother offended is more unyielding than a strong city, and quarreling is like the bars of a castle.*
>
> **Proverbs 18:19**

COMMENTARY:

From Garry: This proverb warns us of the power of offending our brother. The invisible walls of estrangement are hard to tear down. When there is abuse or strife, the bars go up, and the walls that are erected are not easily torn down.

- The Passion Translation states, "It is easier to conquer a strong city than to win back a friend you have offended. Their walls go up, making it nearly impossible to win them back," (Proverbs 18:19 [TPT]).
- The Good News Translation says, "Help your relatives and they will protect you like a strong city wall, but if you quarrel with them, they will close their doors to you," (Proverbs 18:19 [GNT]).
- The Septuagint renders it like this: "A brother helped is like a stronghold, but disputes are like bars of a citadel," (Proverbs 18:19 [LXX]).

In my journal, I reflected on the importance of close relationships. You can strengthen your relationship with a brother if you help him and do not offend him or quarrel with him. Relationships are strong and can go in either direction- they can be strengthened and protected, or if attacked, they can be hard to repair.

From Ward: Being offended today almost seems like a hobby. Various people are quickly offended in social media, and I wonder if this is accurate. We should not seek to offend others. Also, we must be careful not to strike out at those who may have offended us. Here are some quotes about being offended.

- "Being offended by freedom of speech should never be justification for violence," (Alan Dershowitz).
- "An offended heart is the breeding ground for deception," (John Bevere).
- "We have reached a point where people are afraid to talk about what they want to say, because someone might be offended. We have got to get over this sensitivity for it keeps people from saying what they really believe," (Ben Carson).
- "Offense is no longer defense—it's a full-time profession," (Karan Johar).
- "To be offended is a choice we make; it is not a condition inflicted or imposed upon us by someone or something else," (David A. Bednar).

Let us all remember that we should refrain from useless quarreling and deliberately offending others. Community peace remains because of peaceful words.

From Kyle: The following excerpt came from the website *Let God Be True* and seems à propos here. (https://letgodbetrue.com/proverbs/index/chapter-18/proverbs-18-19/):

> Guard all your friendships and relationships carefully. Keep peace with great diligence. Avoid every disagreement and offense that you possibly can. If you cannot avoid them all, then settle them quickly. But be especially careful with those you are closest to.
> The proverb seems extreme. Is it this difficult to reconcile with an offended brother? Is there so little hope of recovery once a close relationship is damaged? Strong cities are seldom taken, and castle bars are of the strongest sort. Solomon's inspired wisdom teaches that once you offend a brother, you are near a hopeless situation. Lord, have mercy!

The proverb is a natural law. It does not justify godly men being slow to forgive their offenders. Nor does it justify godly men giving up the pursuit of a wounded brother. A spiritual man does not live by natural laws. He lives by the Spirit of God, which teaches him to be slow to wrath and quick to forgive (Col 3:12-13; Jas 1:19).

From Cynthia: When I have been right, I have never gotten very far in insisting that I was right. How many wars could be averted if people had put aside revengeful speech? Friends and family have told me how I could have said something better. I usually put my foot in my mouth when I'm caught off guard. A woman once shared that she was sorry for saying something to me. All I could come up with was, "You're just like that—it's the way you are." I didn't mean it rudely, but she took it that way. I was asked to resign shortly after that unfortunate encounter. Maybe we just shouldn't talk until we think about our answer.

From Frank: The relationship with a friend or family member who has been offended is often difficult to mend. Quarreling with them imprisons both you and them emotionally.

From Cindi: Thankfulness for good friends and strong family ties is so very important! I have struggled with staying inside the citadel, where it's safe! God has helped me overcome this tendency, but it tempts me at times. Focusing on others rather than self brings countless blessings!

From Doreen: This is quite true. I've seen it in action. Sometimes, it's easier to forgive friends than it is to forgive family.

PRAYER:

Lord, help me realize how important family and friendships are. Help me protect them and not offend or do damage. Amen.

CHALLENGE:

Be careful in all your relationships to keep the lines of communication open.

_____
_____
_____
_____
_____
_____
_____

THE POWER OF OUR WORDS

 TODAY'S PASSAGE:

> *From the fruit of a man's mouth his stomach is satisfied; he is satisfied by the yield of his lips. Death and life are in the power of the tongue, and those who love it will eat its fruits.*
>
> Proverbs 18:20-21

COMMENTARY:

From Garry: The words we speak are powerful in their effect. So, we need to be careful about what we say and how we say it. Where does our speech come from? Jesus said that what we say comes from what is in our heart. So, the condition of our heart is significant. Proverbs teaches us it is important to speak words that are honest and true. We should not have too many words because "When words are many, transgression is not lacking, but whoever restrains his lips is prudent," (Proverbs 10:19 [ESV]).

Wise words will be calm. This will allow time for a fair hearing, allow tempers to cool, and can be powerful in its effect. Wise words will also be appropriate, and words that match the specific situation will be used. James's letter stresses the power of the tongue and encourages looking to God for wisdom in how to use words to bless others.

From Ward: It is easy to forget that my words have any influence on another person. I have little confidence in my physical skills. I am not a craftsman and am not coordinated in sports. So, the items I repair or make often look like someone from the fourth grade has completed the project. My seventh-grade shop class wooden book holder may have been mistaken for an alien spacecraft.

This same image is transferred to the words I write and speak. Since I did not supervise anyone when I worked, my opinions at my job were equal to those of my co-workers.

Thus, I forget that any words I spoke could affect others. All the words we speak can never be unspoken. Harsh words said in a harsh tone can ruin a relationship.

However, we can disagree without being disagreeable. We can tell others we are angry without belittling them, condemning them, and rejecting them. This takes practice. And part of the practice is sometimes not to speak at all if we are feeling an intense negative emotion.

Encouraging and comforting words can sustain a person in life. Mark Twain wrote, "I can live two months on a good compliment." A wise Methodist pastor, Charles Thompson, once said, "I have learned you should always leave loved ones with loving words." I have remembered this for many years and hopefully have practiced this.

Sometimes, I get angry and say harsh words. I regret these times and wish I could ask for forgiveness from everyone I have spoken to this way. My hope is that the readers of this book may be remembered as persons who always spoke loving and uplifting words. The author of these verses would be pleased.

From Leslie: Good word.

From Doreen: This passage warns about the importance of thinking before speaking.

From Frank: Amen! I firmly believe that the old saying, "Sticks and stones may break my bones, but words will never hurt me," is just wrong.

From Cindi: Cruel words spoken to me years ago have been difficult for me to forget. Unfortunately, I can also remember times when my words hurt someone else. Only with Jesus' forgiveness and love can we heal our past hurts. Only with a Savior can we tame our mouths!

From Cynthia: We don't have to say our thoughts just because we think them. I think many of us would be stoned to death if we lived in some countries that restrict speech. Reading the Word and worshiping Jesus help discipline our speech. Grandchildren help us be better parents with our speech, too. Our culture has so much that isn't worth exposing to our children, and we see this clearly when talking to grandchildren. In Jon Acuff's book, *Soundtracks*, we learn we can control our thoughts so we can have a better day. We can let the good thoughts be louder than our negative thoughts. Fear fuels negativity. Love casts out all fear.

PRAYER:

Lord, guard my mouth. May Your Holy Spirit in my heart produce the fruit of self-control in my speech. Amen.

CHALLENGE:

Use what you say to be a blessing to others.

_____
_____
_____
_____
_____
_____
_____

A GREAT TREASURE

 **TODAY'S PASSAGE:**

He who finds a wife finds a good thing and obtains favor from the LORD.
Proverbs 18:22

COMMENTARY:

From Garry: Marriage is a blessing from God. From the very beginning, when God created the earth, God noticed that while all creation was good. But when He noticed that the man was alone, He said that was not good. So, God created woman, to be a helper fit for the man. When the man saw God's incredible creation of the woman, he was overjoyed!

Genesis 2:24 (ESV) says, "Therefore a man shall leave his father and his mother and hold fast to his wife, and they shall become one flesh." Marriage is a beautiful gift from God.

Proverbs 31:10-12 (ESV) says, "An excellent wife who can find? She is far more precious than jewels. The heart of her husband trusts in her, and he will have no lack of gain. She does him good, and not harm, all the days of her life."

Proverbs 18:22 (TPT) says, "When a man finds a wife, he has found a treasure! For she is the gift of God to bring him joy and pleasure." The Hebrew word for *good* means enjoyable and fortunate. Obtaining favor from the Lord describes that which is pleasing to God, beneficial for life, and abundantly enjoyable. I am so thankful I have found such a good wife! Cindy and I continue to experience joy in our marriage of 47 years!

From Ward: In ancient times, many marriages were arranged. In smaller villages or family groups, marriages were often between relatives. Thus, the man and the woman would have known each other many years before the actual wedding. Family elders believed they knew what personality traits produced the healthiest relationships. So, they would match people based on complementary attributes.

The contemporary interpretation of the past perceives the woman as being bought or sold. But this did not happen in godly communities. Young people trusted their parents to make wise decisions for them that enabled future happiness. The author of this proverb celebrates that, of all the eligible women in the community, the family elders found the best future mate for him.

After the ancient era passed, Western culture became less family-centered and less God-centered, too. Arranged marriages were now viewed as roadblocks to developing romantic love in a relationship. Physical attraction became the main dictator of a successful marriage. This ignores the fact that physical attributes change and often deteriorate over time, while inner character can grow and mature in a healthy marriage relationship.

Today, in Western culture, marriage does not hold the same high value it once did. Since prenuptial agreements exist, quick divorce is available, and cohabitation is required before a marriage ceremony. These current general standards display that marriage is not meant to be a total commitment between the man and the woman. They also imply there is a time limit for how long the legal entity exists. This was never God's intention for a marriage.

In ancient times, the wedding feast was the final celebration. The entire community was excited about the marriage because the whole community had already given approval and input for the engagement. I desire for our culture to rediscover and understand each other's strengths and weaknesses, which is a better indicator of a successful marriage than good looks. The writer of this proverb understands this. There will be favor from the Lord as a couple knows each other well, knows good ways to resolve conflict, and enjoys spending time together. May all those married couples reading this book find goodness in their relationship.

From Wright: Yes.

From Doreen: My husband treats me like a princess, and I am blessed. I work hard to be a good wife. Thankfully, I'm married to my best friend.

From John: God richly blessed me when he placed my wife in my life. I am so thankful we could make it to 50 years of blessed and fruitful marriage. She taught me, through her perfect example, how to be a Christian and how to love everyone unconditionally. Without her guidance and example, I would not be the man I am today; it is all because of her tireless example of how to be "Just Like Jesus."

From Cynthia: We don't have to say our thoughts just because we think them. I think many of us would be stoned to death if we lived in some countries that restrict speech. Reading the Word and worshiping Jesus help discipline our speech. Grandchildren help us be better parents with our speech, too. Our culture has so much that isn't worth exposing to our children, and we clearly see it when talking to grandchildren.

In Jon Acuff's book *Soundtracks*, we learn we can learn to control our own thoughts so we can have a better day. We can let the good thoughts be louder than our negative thoughts. Great marriages are works of art crafted from love and time to inspire others to do better. I can spend an hour enjoying watching great ballerinas and ice-skating couples, and I can spend days contemplating what makes a beautiful marriage. I'm in awe of the craftsmanship some people strive for in their marriages.

PRAYER:

Lord, thank You for my sweet wife. I have truly found a great treasure! Amen.

CHALLENGE:

A wife is a wonderful treasure.

_____
_____
_____
_____
_____
_____

THE RICH AND THE POOR

 **TODAY'S PASSAGE:**

The poor use entreaties, but the rich answer roughly.

Proverbs 18:23

COMMENTARY:

From Garry: Some proverbs are observations about the realities of human behavior. In this proverb, the poor and the rich are contrasted. The poor have needs, and their position is low. They have little leverage. They can let their need be known, but whether help is coming is questionable.

The rich tend to think they have all their needs supplied through their wealth. They can be harsh with the poor, either out of their arrogance or because they view the poor as inferior. They might view the poor as causing their own state of poverty. Sometimes, wealth can make some rude and even cruel in the way they treat less fortunate people. The world can be ugly and harsh. People can be heartless in the way they respond to one another.

Perhaps this proverb indirectly implies our need to be humble and kind to the less fortunate, especially if we have an abundance of possessions.

From Ward: Have you ever been poor? I mean, really poor? Many of us have been broke, and we have no money in our bank accounts and only a few dollars in our pockets. Yet, we may still have a job and a place to live. But have you been poor? I mean, the kind of poor where your resources are so low that there is no one to help you, no permanent place to live, no job, and you're not sure when you will eat again. As this proverb states, the poor must beg for help. This is real poverty.

Repeating the sentence I wrote in the previous devotion, God never intended for anyone to be destitute and without resources to survive. How did our world get into this situation? Our world has wandered far from God's path. The focus of our mind is our personal happiness, and we ignore anyone who is not the same as us.

God has provision for the poor, and the provision is mostly from our own resources. God wants his children to help the poor and not forget they exist. We have few totally destitute in our nation. Mostly, those people are from nations far away. So, if we do not watch the news, we can blame their situation on someone else. Jesus said we will always have the poor around us, but He never said this was the same person this year as last year.

I invite you to write on the lines at the end of this devotion some ways you can assist the poor through prayer, giving, and volunteer work. Also, consider supporting those programs and entities that truly help the poor, not just make the administrators wealthy. God evaluates the sincerity of our faith in how we deal with the helpless. Not by how generous we are to those who have the same economic level as ourselves. This proverb reminds us not to be rough to those not in the same economic circle as we are. This is a wise warning indeed.

From Cindi: Open our eyes, Lord, and show us how You want us to share our many blessings.

From Doreen: This is a sad reality. I've had people advise against my helping a homeless person, who often lingers around my previous workplace. I told them I followed the prompting of the Holy Spirit and let God handle the rest. People helped me a lot when I went through a financially tough time in my life. I know what it means to swallow my pride and ask for help.

From Cynthia: Wealth is relative. Compared to God, we are all poor, but with God, we share in His abundance. The rules of the world seem to change with different rulers over different decades. The rules of the world are complicated and predatory. God operates out of love. God does not profit from our greed. Everyone needs respect and the love of Jesus. Everyone. I would not want to be lacking the love of God when I meet Him face to face. Wealth comes and goes. Great nations abdicate to other nations. We keep our eyes on the prize and help the poor every chance we get. The world is watching.

I'm in awe of those who influence the wealthy to be better people. Jesus said it was nearly impossible, but with God, all things are possible. Some wealthy people don't see that their lifestyle is parasitic in nature. As their wealth multiplies, the poor suffer from neglect. There is a sense of shame for the poor who don't like to be treated as parasites.

PRAYER:

Lord, help me be sympathetic to the needs of the poor and not judge them harshly. Amen.

CHALLENGE:

Be generous and kind, seeking to understand the needs of the poor.

_____
_____
_____
_____
_____
_____
_____

A TRUE FRIEND

 **TODAY'S PASSAGE:**

A man of many companions may come to ruin, but there is a friend who sticks closer than a brother.

Proverbs 18:24

COMMENTARY:

From Garry: This proverb contrasts two levels of friendship. One level is just on the surface, not very deep. They are casual friendships. However, the second description is of a true friend who is close. A good friend in Proverbs is a constant friend who always loves, regardless of the situation. He is constant. A good friend expresses a candid concern. Faithful are the wounds of a friend. It is not flattery but a straightforward concern, even if it is a tough matter. A good friend offers counsel, even if there are differences.

Last of all, a good friend shows tact and respect for another's feelings. Close friendships need to be guarded. Good friends express thoughtfulness, confidence, trust, and integrity. The Message Bible says, "Friends come, and friends go, but a true friend sticks by you like family," (Proverbs 18:24 [MSG]). Some friendships do not last for long, but there is one loving friend who is joined to your heart, closer than any other.

From Ward: Garry's description of a friend is great. I cannot describe a friendship better. But not everyone in our nation has real friends. Current research shows that one out of every seven men has no friends at all. For men in America, many of our friendships are casual and on a surface level. Only 25 percent report having deep friendships. Why is this so? Friendships require time and vulnerability. Our American culture encourages men to be tough and solve their struggles alone. An intimate emotional connection with a person of the same sex protects our mental health and helps us deal with stress.

Is there anything we can do if we know a person of the same sex as us has no friends? Judy Yi-Chung Chu, a lecturer from Stanford University, recommends:

- Start with a simple invitation to coffee or a bite to eat.
- Invite the person to have a fun activity with you.
- Ask meaningful questions.
- Listen and display genuine sincerity. The other person is not a project for you.
- Share your own vulnerability.
- Sometimes, it is easier not to look each other in the face.

Everyone wants friends, but not all know how to develop deep friendships. I encourage the reader to nurture devoted friendships and to be kind and gracious to those who have no friends.

From Doreen: Most people have close friends who they call their chosen family. Friends are very important for life, health, and happiness. Even though I tend to be an introvert, I work to strengthen my close relationships.

From Cindi: Thank You, God, for my friends who are a source of joy and support. Most of all, thank You, Jesus, for your friendship, which is my constant counsel and guide.

From Leslie: I always thought of Jesus as a friend who is closer than a brother.

From John: In 2024, I had a year that was one I never thought would happen. I certainly never thought I would go through what I went through caring for my now-late wife. But it happened, and it was finally over in October. Through that experience, I found out how many *true* friends I really had. Many just seemed to disappear, but when I saw them, they would usually tell me to let them know if I needed their help.

On the other hand, I had a few friends who would call me regularly. They would come by my home to check on me to see if there was anything they could do for me. The calls and the visits were more than enough. Those who called and visited have not stopped, and I do not feel like they will. I am inspired to do the same for people I know who are going through a tough time in their lives. Loyal friends are few, but they become many when you need them.

From Cynthia: It's taken me several years to be a better friend. At times, I felt like Jesus was the only One who listened to me—Who really got me. "What a friend we have in Jesus...." He doesn't half listen and is teaching me to be a better listener. The advent of mobile devices has weakened many relationships because it's tough to be rejected by a phone. I would rather have a staring contest every single day with my loved ones than have competition with mobile devices.

From Frank: A true friend is a great treasure.

PRAYER:

Lord, help me be a true friend to those who are close to me. Amen.

CHALLENGE:

Be a friend who is loyal and trustworthy.

_____
_____
_____
_____
_____
_____

INTEGRITY IS BETTER

 **TODAY'S PASSAGE:**

Better is a poor person who walks in his integrity than one who is crooked in speech and is a fool.

Proverbs 19:1

COMMENTARY:

From Garry: Who you are is more important than what you have. Integrity and honest speech are better than deception or manipulation. Truthfulness is a vital and primary virtue in Proverbs. In our society today, a term used often is *compulsive liar*. Some people lie so often they are out of touch with reality. That is so sad.

As I thought about what I might write about this proverb, I also thought about the poor. Being poor might be an outward condition, but it does not need to define who you are on the inside. I asked myself: "What does the rest of this chapter say about the poor? A similar verse is Proverbs 19:22 (ESV): "What is desired in a man is steadfast love, and a poor man is better than a liar."

However, being poor has a downside. Proverbs 19:7 (ESV) says, "All a poor man's brothers hate him; how much more do his friends go far from him! He pursues them with words but does not have them." Proverbs 19:4 (ESV) says, "Wealth brings many new friends, but a poor man is deserted by his friend." Poverty might affect your relationships and your ability to make an impact with the limited resources you have.

But you can still be generous with what you have, and there is a benefit to being generous, especially to those in need. Proverbs 19:17 (ESV) states, "Whoever is generous to the poor lends to the LORD, and he will repay him for his deed."

From Ward: We live in a world where people say words they do not mean and do actions they later regret. Integrity is not a word I hear repeatedly. Our culture accepts that a person will present different personalities in separate situations.

My father was this way. He was a traveling salesperson for many years, so he would often talk on the phone at home. I saw he acted one way with his customers, one way with his family, and a third way at church. He did not trust what others said. Often, he would say aloud, "I wonder what he meant by saying that?" These different personas seemed to cause him much stress. He displayed anger at home towards his family. I think this stemmed from the stress caused by his different behavior outside the home. After leaving home, I realized that adapting my personality to different situations was not God's plan for us.

Integrity means being one person all the time. And for some folks, this is tough. How can someone become a person of integrity?

- Be honest in what you say and do.
- Be responsible for your words and actions.
- Respect yourself and others.
- Be patient with others and with yourself.
- Remember to say, "Thank you."
- Be compassionate with all.

These traits may not be easy for some to do. I encourage the reader each week to take one of these attributes and make it a part of their life. I believe integrity will grow inside you.

From Cynthia: Wealth can bring a new set of problems. I've never been wealthy financially, but there is some bliss when you're broke. No one borrows money from you, and rarely are you asked to attend parties. You can always respond with, "It's not in the budget," when you aren't interested. People are blessed when they can help you, and there is a certain level of humility that goes with accepting help. People usually like to repay kindness by helping other people.

My mother was content after her stroke. She couldn't remember the problems of the world and had a clean conscience. She never told lies, and she never said bad words. The Bible also says to refrain from talking more than necessary, but I'm still working on that one.

It's disappointing when we turn our power over to liars. No one wants to be taken advantage of, but they rarely think they might be part of the problem. Seeking the truth by accepting the gift of discernment will protect us. Seeking God's Truth before we make any substantial decision is ideal.

From Doreen: There are many verses from Proverbs I've seen played out in my life or the lives of people I know. For instance, I know a person who was poor because of their foolishness. Although they had some virtuous traits, they kept digging a deeper hole by continuing to make bad choices. I also know another person who is poor but has integrity.

There is a rude businessperson I am familiar with who treats disadvantaged customers poorly and the "known" rich customers much more respectfully. This person talks badly about the poor customers, which ultimately makes them look bad. As a result, the business has lost customers.

There have been a few periods in my life where I had little money, but I still maintained my integrity. At one point, I made some decisions out of desperation to get out of an unpleasant situation, of which I'm not proud. God sent some people to help me through those difficult times. I now try to help others when I can, and I don't look down on disadvantaged people.

PRAYER:

Lord, may I have integrity in everything I say and do. You place great value on the truth, and so should I. Help me be truthful, Lord. Amen.

CHALLENGE:

Truth is important, and so is generosity.

_____
_____
_____
_____
_____
_____
_____

NO RUSH

TODAY'S PASSAGE:

> *Desire without knowledge is not good, and whoever makes haste with his feet misses his way.*
>
> **Proverbs 19:2**

COMMENTARY:

From Garry: Being careful and being aware is a good way to approach life. Just rushing ahead blindly usually gets you into trouble. The Passion Translation says today's passage this way: "The best way to live is with revelation-knowledge, for without it, you'll grow impatient and run right into error," (Proverbs 19.2 [TPT]). The Complete Jewish Bible says, "To act without knowing how you function is not good; and if you rush ahead, you will miss your goal," (Proverbs 19:2 [CJB]).

In my journal, I wrote to "be aware, be careful, don't rush, think it through." "Know what you are doing!" Otherwise, you will trip up, especially if you do not think and instead hurry right into a mistake. Have you ever assembled a piece of furniture? I have made the mistake of rushing ahead of the step-by-step instructions more than once and paying for it. The same is true in life.

From Ward: Ever since I became an adult, I have been in a hurry. I believed I had many tasks to do, and they each had to be accomplished by a certain time. This resulted in much stress and exhaustion. Moreover, the list of tasks for each week seemed to grow longer, not shorter.

Only recently have I realized that few chores must be done quickly. Hurry can cause me to make mistakes. I am more peaceful when I add rest to my daily schedule. For the ancients, running was only for slaves. Since everyone walked, being in a hurry wasted their strength, a strength that needed to be saved for the rest of the journey.

In our daily culture, many people encourage the public to hurry, to be first in line, and to race to the finish line. Let us not be manipulated by the promoters of *hurry* when the accomplishment is not to our benefit but only theirs. Quietness and rest can provide more peace than a completed checklist of tasks we have completed. Here are some quotes about hurry that you may appreciate:

- There is a Finnish proverb that says, "God did not invent hurry."
- Livy wrote, "All things will be clear and distinct to the man who does not hurry."
- Bruce Feiler wrote, "When you hurry, you get where you are going, but you get there alone."
- Robert Louis Stevenson wrote, "He who sows hurry, reaps indigestion."

From Frank C: Great advice and wisdom.

From Frank H: Don't be impulsive; haste makes waste.

From Doreen: First, pray about whatever choice you are facing to find out if that's what you should do. Then, research what you want to do before following through with your plans. I've learned from experience that it's the best route.

From Cindi: For many years, I believed that the more I could cram into my to-do list, the better! This resulted in doing a whole lot of activities, all mediocre and without a sense of tranquility ever! I rushed through so many years. As an older adult, I so clearly see that God didn't intend for us to run around like our hair's on fire! I accomplished a lot of things but missed out on being still and knowing God more. Thank You, Jesus, for this time in life and for this opportunity.

From Cynthia: When I didn't listen to good advice and did what I wanted to save time, I regretted my decision. Dallas Willard said, "You need to ruthlessly eliminate hurry from your life." He was also heard to say, "Hurry is the devil."

Hoarding, lack of time management, and being too busy come from a lack of vision. Hurrying is a by-product of poor boundaries and misuse of our resources. Hurrying can result in being too busy to:

- Go to church.
- Pray/self-reflect.
- Learn gratitude.
- Be with family.

Good leaders really listen. Good leaders pause. Great leaders worship Jesus. Jesus' very example was of patience, peacefulness, and love.

PRAYER:

Father, help me be a careful, thoughtful person who is not in a rush. Amen.

CHALLENGE:

Slow down and think about it.

_____
_____
_____
_____
_____
_____
_____

BLAMING GOD

 **TODAY'S PASSAGE:**

When a man's folly brings his way to ruin, his heart rages against the LORD.
Proverbs 19:3

COMMENTARY:

From Garry: When life gets messed up, there is a human tendency to want to blame God rather than accept responsibility for our actions. God gets blamed for what we bring on ourselves.

- The International Children's Bible says, "A person's own foolishness ruins his life. But in his mind, he blames the Lord for it," (Proverbs 19:3 [ICB]).
- The Passion Translation says, "There are some people who ruin their own lives and then blame it all on God," (Proverbs 19:3 [TPT]).

Part of the human problem is blaming God. All the way back to the beginning, in the Garden of Eden, the woman blamed the serpent, and the man blamed the woman. The natural tendency is to blame someone else. But we need to accept responsibility for our actions.

- The Contemporary English Version says, "We are ruined by our own stupidity, though we blame the LORD," (Proverbs 19:3 [CEV]).
- J. Paul Getty said, "A man may fail many times, but he isn't a failure until he begins to blame somebody else."

From Ward: When I was younger, I would often blame God for the stressful events in my life. I thought, *God is sovereign, so He must have some responsibility for the mess I am in.* However, God corrected me. After teaching in a public junior high for three years, I was tired and overwhelmed. I was not happy with my job. I prayed to God, lamenting my situation. I reminded God that he had called me to teach, and now I believed I was a failure. I did not know if I should continue to teach or seek another job.

Then, the Lord spoke clearly in my mind. He said, "I never called you to teach. You chose to do that. Stop blaming me for your choices. I can bless you if you teach. I can bless you if you do not teach. But you decide." The conversation continued for a few minutes. God reminded me I must be mature and accept responsibility for my choices. And not to take my thoughts and ideas and turn them into a specific Word from God. I realized how many Christians will do this. I saw my relationship with Him was going to be different. He was not going to give orders, and I would obey with no conversation.

I learned that a sincere relationship with God was a continual conversation each day. God is my Father, but he is not my boss. As I daily talk with God and receive his input, the decisions for my life become joint decisions. I should not choose worry, doubt, or fear. I do not need to be angry, knowing God has only good for me, if I just listen.

Life has been more comfortable since that conversation many years ago. I am pleased that Father God broke through the thoughts in my mind to assure me of his concern and care for me. And telling me what walking with Jesus was like each day. May everyone reading this book hear the Lord clearly about His love and compassion for you.

From Cynthia: A good portion of my life has been spent blaming others and sometimes God. At least once, I've wrestled with God, particularly when a good friend lost her daughter to cancer a few months after her baby was born. This event came a few days after her other daughter got married. It wasn't fair. My friend did everything right. I thought God should have rewarded her.

God loves us and is patient with our hearts. God has so many lessons that we miss if we harden our hearts.

One day, someone reminded me of my blessings, and then I heard several great sermons on forgiveness. I decided I'd rather please God, make the right decisions, and respond how He would want so His face would shine on me.

From Leslie: In the movie *Dead Man Walking*, Susan Sarandon plays a nun who is ministering to Sean Penn. He is on death row for murdering two young people and is blaming everybody for his actions. She looks at him and asks him, "Where were you in all of this?"

The first part of becoming a believer in Christ is admitting that we are sinners and at fault. That's why we need a Savior.

From John: We as humans think we know what we are doing, only to discover our plans have flaws we did not recognize. Then, we try to rationalize our failure. We find outside reasons for the failure and do not think we were at fault. With the growth of faith, we do a better job of thinking through our future actions.

I go to the Lord in prayer and then look in Scripture to see what God thinks. Then, things typically work smoother, and I can rejoice in my success by thanking the Lord for His help.

From Barrett: Today's passage brings to mind a famous quote by Abraham Lincoln. He states, "My great concern is not whether you have failed, but whether you are content with your failure." Being content with failure brings with it the ruin mentioned in today's proverb. Raging against God implies that personal failure is the fault of someone or something else.

We are witnessing this today. News reports, redolent with excuses, lies, and new discoveries, appear in the media regarding the tragic fires on the West Coast. The one thing California officials glaringly lack is any shadow of personal responsibility. They lack responsibility for any of the wrong decisions and resulting failures they made, all the while raging against the facts and God's truth.

From Cindi: In my house, "Not Me" did everything that wasn't right! Busy fellow....

PRAYER:

Lord, help me accept responsibility for my actions and admit when I am wrong. Amen.

CHALLENGE:

Be responsible and have the courage to face the truth. Don't blame God.

_____
_____
_____
_____
_____
_____
_____

BEING A FRIEND

 **TODAY'S PASSAGE:**

Wealth brings many new friends, but a poor man is deserted by his friend.
Proverbs 19:4

COMMENTARY:

From Garry: In my journal, I reflected that this verse shows people tend to pursue wealthy people, hoping they can get a share of the pie. However, the poor are shunned because the wealthy are afraid that the poor will try to gain something from them.

Look carefully at a cluster of proverbs that deal with wealth, poverty, and relationships:

- Proverbs 18:23,24 (ESV). states, "The poor use entreaties, but the rich answer roughly. A man of many companions may come to ruin, but there is a friend who sticks closer than a brother."
- Proverbs 19:6,7 (ESV) says, "Many seek the favor of a generous man, and everyone is a friend to a man who gives gifts. All a poor man's brothers hate him; how much more do his friends go far from him! He pursues them with words but does not have them."

Wealth has power, and when combined with generosity, it can influence people. Yet people are basically selfish, and wealth may create "friends," but they may be shallow friendships. Poverty has little power and rarely attracts interest. Faithful relationships are what really matter.

From Ward: This proverb is difficult for me to understand. I thought the poor, the wealthy, and everyone in between had friends. I looked at the Hebrew for this verse, and the words are "The wealthy add many associates; the poor is parted from his associates."

I think the writer is hinting that one reason for poverty is that the destitute have been abandoned or ignored by their neighbors. This should never be and is never God's intention for anyone he has created. God is a community of the Father, the Son, and the Holy Spirit. He wants all people on the earth to be part of a community, too. When we are separated from any community, our ability to continue to have abundance is insecure.

As an introvert, having close friends has not always been easy. Yet, I still see the need to maintain close friendships. Not only does this bring joy, but it also allows me to have a balanced view of life. Those folks who have no friends are in a poor state of existence. True faithful friends bring comfort, information, stability, encouragement, hope, and possible help. Friendships take time—time to build and time to maintain. And the outcome is worth the time. Let us pray for those we know who have no friends and that others will reach out to develop positive relationships with them.

From Doreen: This is sad but true. In my experience, many people are very judgmental of poor people. I can include myself in that statement. I know some people who live with a very low income, who are poor because of their chronic bad choices. I also know a handicapped homeless man whom I helped a lot. He lived in poverty and became homeless because of several circumstances out of his control during Hurricane Rita.

I also know that people who are rich or live a comfortable life are judged and sometimes targeted. We became estranged from some family members who manipulated and took advantage of us for years. They were friendly with us because we helped them. However, they got upset when we quit helping them because of addictions they refused to address. Both situations have given me a great deal of wisdom.

From Cynthia: Paul was content. I admire people who can be content in both good and bad circumstances, whether they are poor or wealthy, and in all their relationships. Nehemiah is another person who looked for the good that could be done when the community was reconstructed to bring glory to God.

PRAYER:

Lord, thank You for all the ways You have blessed me materially. May I be a faithful and generous friend. Amen.

CHALLENGE:

Relationship matters.

_____
_____
_____
_____
_____
_____
_____

BE TRUTHFUL

TODAY'S PASSAGE:

> *A false witness will not go unpunished, and he who breathes out lies will not escape. A false witness will not go unpunished, and he who breathes out lies will perish.*
>
> **Proverbs 19:5, 9**

COMMENTARY:

From Garry: Perjury is the offense of willfully telling an untruth in a court after having taken the oath to tell the truth. The truth is so important because you cannot have justice without it. We can see it in the ninth commandment of the Ten Commandments. Exodus 20:16 (ESV) says, "You shall not bear false witness against your neighbor." Honesty and truth help settle a matter.

Proverbs 14:25 (ESV) says, "A truthful witness saves lives, but one who breathes out lies is deceitful." Falsehood and lies twist and distort in such a way that our neighbor is hurt. If lies abound, you will be found out. Injustice occurs when the truth is ignored. God made us for community, but community cannot function rightly if the truth is not made known.

From Ward:
What are some frequent lies you may hear? Please take a moment and write a few on the lines at the end of this devotion. Here are some I have heard:
- Yes, I floss every day.
- No, Officer, I did not know I was speeding.
- I'm fine. Nothing's wrong.
- I don't lie.
- What about lies Christians may say?

- I pray every day.
- I don't have enough time to read the Bible.
- I'll pray about that.
- I don't need to be around other Christians to be a Christian.

If we trust one another and believe others sincerely love us, we have no reason to lie. Telling the truth means you trust the person you are talking to. Jesus never lied and set an example for us. God does not hold truth; He is truth. His very being is truth. When we speak the truth and act truthfully, we are being one with God the Father and with Jesus the Son.

When we lie, we break our oneness with God and with the Christian community. These proverbs remind us that lies never last and liars will be revealed. Let us not adopt the world's image that lying is just a part of our daily work. Let us live with truth so that God's goodness can be displayed to the world.

From Frank: I think it was a Mark Twain quote that said, "Always tell the truth; it will gratify some and astonish the rest."

From Doreen: If you tell the truth, you won't have to remember the story that you made up or who you lied to. One of the hardest things about having a parent with dementia is lying to them to keep them from getting upset over things they forgot.

From Barrett: This famous quote seems à propos:

> *We know they are lying. They know they are lying. They know that we know that they are lying. We know that they know that we know that they know they are lying. And still…they continue to lie.*
> **Aleksandr Solzhenitsyn**

From Cynthia: How can we point the way to Jesus if we are lying to others? How can we be on the side of justice if we lie? A vibrant life is based on Truth. Jesus is the Truth and the

Way. Jesus is the life worth living for. I ask forgiveness for falling short of the Truth in so many ways.

From Cindi: Some of my most trying times have been because of others' lies. I'm so glad I walk with Jesus, Who never lies, always keeps His promises, and helps me live in truth.

PRAYER:

Lord, help me be utterly truthful in all I say and do. Amen.

CHALLENGE:

Always tell the truth.

_____
_____
_____
_____
_____
_____
_____

DISCOVERING GOOD

 **TODAY'S PASSAGE:**

Whoever gets sense loves his own soul; he who keeps understanding will discover good.

Proverbs 19:8

COMMENTARY:

From Garry: See the following translations for today's passage:

- The Complete Jewish Bible says: "To acquire good sense is to love oneself; to treasure discernment is to prosper," (Proverbs 19:8 [CJB]).
- The Good News Translation states: "Do yourself a favor and learn all you can; then remember what you learn and you will prosper," (Proverbs 19:8 [GNT]).
- The Message Bible puts it this way: "Grow a wise heart—you'll do yourself a favor; keep a clear head—you'll find a good life," (Proverbs 19:8 [MSG]).

Getting *sense* is getting a mind that works well. It is a way of the heart that exhibits a clear understanding. When you understand God's ways, you find fulfillment and purpose. But just knowing without putting what you know into practice is not enough. Following through with a proper understanding leads to the greater good. Consider:

And now, O sons, listen to me: blessed are those who keep my ways. Hear instruction and be wise, and do not neglect it. Blessed is the one who listens to me, watching daily at my gates, waiting beside my doors. For whoever finds me

> *finds life and obtains favor from the LORD, but he who fails to find me injures himself; all who hate me love death.*
>
> **Proverbs 8:32-36 (ESV)**

A final thought related to today's passage comes from Proverbs 15:

> *Whoever ignores instruction despises himself, but he who listens to reproof gains intelligence. The fear of the LORD is instruction in wisdom, and humility comes before honor.*
>
> **Proverbs 15:32-33 (ESV)**

From Ward:
The word "sense" in this proverb can also be translated as "wisdom." Alas, in today's culture, people do not seem to want good sense or wisdom, but they want someone to agree with their opinion. How far we have walked away from seeking eternal insight and instead seek validation for our thoughts. As our population expands, so do the philosophies that want to explain our existence. God's perspective on life does not seem to be an option for many in terms of how to deal with conflict and tragedy.

So many turn their face away from God and create fantasies and imaginations as resources for solving struggles. Wisdom is not tough to find. Good sense is not far from us. We can find sensible, workable, godly solutions to all the challenges we face if we explore God's word first. We must clear our minds of trying to justify our current assumptions and think of Godly understanding.

Psalm 119:105 says, "Your word is a lamp to my feet." (NKJV), not the opinion of my best friends. Psalm 37:3 says, "Trust in the Lord.' (NKJV) not in your favorite political leader. This proverb reminds us that we will find good in listening to the Lord and walking in his ways. These are good words for any generation.

From Doreen: This makes total sense. The more wisdom we have, the better decisions we make, and the better our lives will be in the long run.

From Cindi: My mind has calmed, and my inner spirit is more content at this time in my life than my much younger self. How grateful I am to God, Who has loved me through it all!

From Cynthia: There are so many voices trying to gain their place in our hearts and minds. The loudest ones will win. Keeping our eyes on the prize, we must listen to Jesus' voice, the Truth. We can gain wisdom. We can follow through with what we need to do. God has so many good thoughts and plans for us. He has new beginnings and new days full of good gifts. Even in difficult times, God has the time to teach us and mold us. For example, anyone searching for Scripture that matches the popular slogan of the day, *self-care*, will find it in God's Word. The Bible always addresses important concepts related to our daily lives.

PRAYER:

Lord, You are the Author of all that is good. I want to discover Your goodness and live a full and meaningful life. I cannot do it without You, so help me, Lord. Amen.

CHALLENGE:

Get common sense. Get wisdom. Follow through. You will be glad you did.

_____
_____
_____
_____
_____
_____
_____

JARRING ABSURDITIES

 TODAY'S PASSAGE:

> It is not fitting for a fool to live in luxury, much less for a slave to rule over princes.
>
> **Proverbs 19:10**

COMMENTARY:

From Garry: Some proverbs reveal something that should not be. There are several proverbs like this:

- "Like a gold ring in a pig's snout is a beautiful woman without discretion," (Proverbs 11:22 [ESV]).
- "Fine speech is not becoming to a fool; still less is false speech to a prince," (Proverbs 17:7 [ESV]).
- "Like snow in summer or rain in harvest, so, honor is not fitting for a fool," (Proverbs 26:1 [ESV]).
- "Under three things the earth trembles; under four it cannot bear up: a slave when he becomes king, and a fool when he is filled with food; an unloved woman when she gets a husband, and a maidservant when she displaces her mistress," (Proverbs 30:21-23 [ESV]).

There are certain situations that make sense, and when one observes something out of place, it is noticeable.

From Ward: Have you ever been in a job or group where the leader lacks the knowledge or talent to lead? I have. When this happens, there is often some confusion and wondering. In many work situations, a promotion to management **is a reward for loyalty**

and longevity rather than a person showing leadership ability. The proverb warns us not to give a worker tasks that do not fit their expertise. In the last few years, I have noticed that many companies do not adequately train employees for their assigned work. The reasons are varied:

- Co-workers have not been trained, so they cannot train others.
- Supervisors do not have time or a budget for training.
- Upper management views low-level employees as expendable and not worth any training.

What a sad time when some leaders view followers as worthless. Philippians 2:3b (NKJV) says, "Let each esteem others better than himself."

1 Timothy provides instruction about bosses and employees. A leader must be "able to teach" (1 Timothy 3:2b [NKJV]) and must "Not [be] a novice, lest being puffed up with pride he fall..." (1 Timothy 3:6a [NKJV, Emphasis Added]).

Current leaders have the responsibility to train their replacements and not expect the recruit to learn all tasks on their own. In the same way, an untrained and inexperienced person should not be given great responsibility because pride and arrogance develop. May all of us have the talent for the work we have been given. Let us not envy those above us, nor belittle those below us, and do our work with peace and confidence.

From Cynthia: God is all about using lessons to teach us. God is not a God of confusion. Trickery, thieving, and lying to elevate oneself may keep the best person for the position away.

From Doreen: A fool probably doesn't have the wisdom to handle living in luxury. They would squander away the luxuries. A slave wouldn't have the background, wisdom, or education to rule over princes.

From Jim: It is a downhill slope when what should not make sense is touted, advertised, and proclaimed as what is right.

PRAYER:

Lord, may my life be consistent and make sense. Amen.

CHALLENGE:

Live in such a way that there are no glaring contradictions.

LIVING BIG

 **TODAY'S PASSAGE:**

Good sense makes one slow to anger, and it is his glory to overlook an offense.
Proverbs 19:11

COMMENTARY:

From Garry: Living big is living graciously. It is being patient with yourself and with others by not reacting. It is a careful response to others' mistakes. Living big includes the ability to not only forgive but also to shrug off insults. It is passing over an offense and not overreacting by being hypersensitive. It involves having tough skin and self-discipline.

The New Century Version says, "The wise are patient; they will be honored if they ignore insults," (Proverbs 19:11 [NCV]). The Amplified Bible states, "Good sense *and* discretion make a man slow to anger, And it is his honor *and* glory to overlook a transgression *or* an offense [without seeking revenge and harboring resentment]," (Proverbs 19:11 [AMP]).

Rev. Derek Kidner, an ordained Anglican priest, wrote in his commentary on Proverbs:

> The word for glory is sometimes translated "beauty"; it suggests adornment, and so brings out here the glowing colors of a virtue which, in practice, may look drably unassertive. God Himself declares His "Almighty power most chiefly in showing mercy and pity."

From Ward: "Overlook an offense." I have not heard this in over 20 years. Do you ever hear or read these words? In our world today, we cherish any time we are offended so that we may hurl insults at the source of the irritating words. Politeness is out of style. This seems to be the formula for American culture—since the first person was rude and critical, I may act the same way. The New Century Version of this verse says, "The wise

...will be honored if they ignore insults," (Proverbs 19:11 [NCV]). Ignoring an insult does not seem like an option today. Yet, we can receive honor for restraining our words.

Jesus said no harsh words to anyone while going to His death or hanging on the cross. On the contrary, He prayed for His persecutors. We should do the same. Humility should be our aim, not to devise a clever reply to those who oppose us. Wars, animosity, and broken relationships happen when we focus on offenses and transgressions we have received. Jesus did not act that way and pointed us to establish peace in our community and peace within our souls. May all who read this devotion forsake anger and bitter reactions and choose peace instead.

From Frank: Excellent, Garry! I learned about Derek Kinder in just the last year or so from listening to Tim Keller's sermons.

From Cynthia: My favorite places of worship are led by pastors who love their families. I've never met a perfect pastor or person, but I've met those who have a big, big heart. A beautiful church is led by people who point to Jesus. That won't happen if the leaders aren't forgiving or generous with time and resources.

From Cliff: Recently, I messed up and let anger get the best of me during third period. I appreciated the prayers of my friends in Christ to help me going forward.

From Cindi: Honestly, I have struggled with being slow to react when I see or even feel injustice or mistreatment. My emotions are triggered, and I speak out, wanting to right the wrong. God is working in me to not have such emotional responses and to let Him handle things! I rarely help the situation when I do not let Him work. I want to give *Him* glory! Help me, Lord!

From Kelley: Garry, this reminds me so much of one of my favorite Scriptures, James 1:19 (NIV), which says, "My dear brothers and sisters, take note of this: Everyone should be quick to listen, slow to speak and slow to become angry." It's sensible to pause and consider the wisdom of responding thoughtfully to others' words and tone. Many times, it's about perspective; seeing the situation from the other person's perspective will help you understand where they are coming from. This should hopefully lead to a dialogue, rather than an argument. May the Grace and Peace of Jesus Christ be with you.

From Doreen: As I've grown in my faith and maturity, I can see the value in this. Thankfully, God has helped me get a lot better at practicing it as well. Overlooking an offense goes along with forgiveness and not gossiping about the offender to everyone.

PRAYER:

Lord God, You are slow to anger and full of mercy. May I be like You, Lord. Amen

CHALLENGE:

Live graciously. Be patient. Understand that people make mistakes, so forgive them. Live big!

_____
_____
_____
_____
_____
_____

USING POWER FOR GOOD

 **TODAY'S PASSAGE:**

A king's wrath is like the growling of a lion, but his favor is like dew on the grass.

Proverbs 19:12

COMMENTARY:

From Garry: A king is powerful, so do not make him mad. When a king favors you, you are blessed, at least while he is king. Other proverbs speak about a king:

- Proverbs 16:14-15 (ESV) says, "A king's wrath is a messenger of death, and a wise man will appease it. In the light of a king's face there is life, and his favor is like the clouds that bring the spring rain."
- Proverbs 20:2 (ESV) says, "The terror of a king is like the growling of a lion; whoever provokes him to anger forfeits his life."

When you stop and think about it, verse 11 of Proverbs 19 would offer a good word to those in power. It would be good for a leader in authority not only to 'live big' but also to be faithful in administering justice for all. King David was the father of Solomon, and David himself, in his dying words, said in 2 Samuel:

The God of Israel has spoken; the Rock of Israel has said to me: When one rules justly over men, ruling in the fear of God, he dawns on them like the morning light, like the sun shining forth on a cloudless morning, like rain that makes grass to sprout from the earth.

2 Samuel 23:3-4 (ESV)

From Ward: Bible teacher and scholar Jim Flemming has said, "There are few good kings." Kings have a lot of power and mostly use it to enrich themselves and their friends. That is why this proverb reminds us that the king's favor is good for those few who receive it, and most of us generally receive his wrath. Leadership should not be this way.

In the book of Titus, Paul gives us the standard for being a leader. In chapters one and two, he describes an executive as being:

> *blameless - faithful - not self-willed - not violent - just - self-controlled - reverent - sober-minded - holy - loving what is good - having integrity*

Perhaps my view of this world is negative. I see few leaders in any nation of the world having these traits—in government, private industry, education, or non-profits.

This situation is not new. Reading any history of central governments for the last 6000 years shows partiality and corruption appearing in the small group of wealthy leaders. The only groups to show justice, equity, and courtesy to the public have been indigenous peoples who have few possessions, and leadership consists of a rotating group of elders. It is possible to have kind, patient, caring bosses in any group. The commanders must give up selfishness and the desire to control others. They must focus on the good of the community and not their small personal group.

The instructions in Titus from Paul support the possibility of this happening. Our duty is to pray for leaders, public and private, secular and spiritual, to make godliness the focus of our work. The more people who pray this way, the more likely those types of leaders will appear to guide our world. Father, may all Your people pray each day that godly people will be raised up to have authority in our culture.

From Doreen: This is true in work situations as well. I have worked with a supervisor who was harsh with me, for unknown reasons, when I first started at a job. I prayed for God to help me treat that person with respect because they had authority over me. I also prayed for God to help me find favor with this supervisor. God answered my prayer. The difference made my work easier. I still walked on eggshells around them because they had a volatile personality, but it did improve.

From Cynthia: Influencing our leaders is beyond the capability of most. Many times, "anxiety" is the emotion most leaders inspire. I admire the people who inspire leaders to greatness. We must always pray for our leaders in every area of our lives for our children's sake—and for the Glory of God.

From Cindi: It is important to include our leaders in our prayers! They need God's help!

PRAYER:

Lord, thank You for our leaders. Give them understanding, compassion, and justice. Help us as a nation to be supportive so that You are honored. Righteousness exalts a nation. Have mercy, Lord. Amen.

CHALLENGE:

Pray for your President and all those who work with him.

___
___
___
___
___
___
___

PAIN OR PEACE?

 **TODAY'S PASSAGE:**

A foolish son is ruin to his father, and a wife's quarreling is a continual dripping of rain. House and wealth are inherited from fathers, but a prudent wife is from the LORD.

Proverbs 19:13-14

COMMENTARY:

From Garry: An Arab proverb says, "Three things make a house intolerable:

- *tak* (the leaking through of rain)
- *nak* (a wife's nagging) and
- *bak* (bugs)."

The Passion Translation of verses 13 and 14 says,

A rebellious son breaks a father's heart, and a nagging wife can drive you crazy! You can inherit houses and land from your parents, but a good wife only comes as a gracious gift from God!

Proverbs 19:13-14 (TPT)

In my journal, I wrote: "Foolishness, stupidity, and rebellion bring pain to the family." The father, the head of the house, is hurt by the wrong actions of his children, and he is hurt by a wife who nags, nags, nags. It seems to never end! Poor guy!

But in contrast to the pain in verse 13, there is the peace that comes from a prudent, sensible, congenial wife. A wife who has a skillful use of knowledge and discretion blesses the family. She brings peace and stability. Verse 14 affirms that when a marriage works out well, one should credit it as a gift from God.

From Ward: I wonder how many people reading this devotion have a rebellious child or a quarrelsome spouse. Thinking about the couples I know who divorce and families with emotional separation, I suspect many have these circumstances. I feel sad for families where contention and harshness replace love and peace. God never wants a family to experience tension and anger each day. He gives good gifts like an inheritance or a prudent spouse, but not every family seems to receive these gifts.

How can we have a family that is peaceful and succeeds? Is it possible to create a stable family? When searching online, the same ideas appeared on various websites.

- Practice forgiveness, both for ourselves and for others.
- Be willing to apologize. Lily Tomlin once said, "Forgiveness means letting go of any hope for a better past." We must let go of our bitterness and desire to take revenge.
- Be willing to listen to each other. Understanding the other person is sometimes more important than making ourselves understood.
- Have a fun time together.
- Show compassion, thankfulness, and generosity. Everyone appreciates sincere compliments and care.
- Speak with "I" statements instead of "You" statements. Focus on what you want and feel, and not on how the other person should change.
- Realize you do not always know the correct cause, see the accurate observation, and have the proper solution.

I encourage each one of us to try these tasks and see what happens in your family dynamics.

From Cindi: With God's help, Patrick and I will celebrate 39 years of marriage this year. It would have been easy to just gripe about stuff and point out the others' faults! It is much harder to let God work on the partners in marriage so that they grow in their own faith walk and communicate productively to have a happy life. I am so thankful for my husband and for how we have grown together.

From Doreen: Once again, I love Proverbs! This verse is another example of how choices have a ripple effect. Some are small ripples that don't go very far. Others are big ripples that spread out beyond our sight. Some choices affect the lives of others years after they have been made. Many things we do, even small things, impact the lives of others, eventually. Some in a good way, others in a bad way.

A foolish child or a nagging wife can make others miserable. Of course, when I was young and rebellious, I made some choices that gave my parents grief. Thankfully, God helped me learn from my mistakes, and I started making better choices. I have also learned many lessons from seeing how the choices that others have made have affected their life in different ways. Now, I am very aware of how my choices affect the lives of those around me. I'm far from perfect. However, I work to make good choices to make sure I don't cause grief to those around me.

From Wright: I know three men who were really worn down by their wives' nagging.

From Frank: Amen. That is beautifully said and beautifully true.

From John: I was blessed to have a prudent wife for over fifty years. During that time, she literally changed my life and brought me to a love of Jesus; she taught me to love unconditionally. She affected countless lives, and she always had a positive effect on all those she encountered. Thank You, Lord!

PRAYER:

Lord, thank You for our prudent wives. These ladies are gifts to their husbands. Thank You for their wisdom and understanding. And Lord, thank You for our spouses who bless our lives so richly. Amen.

CHALLENGE:

Build a family of faith.

LAZYBONES

 **TODAY'S PASSAGE:**

> *Slothfulness casts into a deep sleep, and an idle person will suffer hunger.*
> **Proverbs 19:15**

COMMENTARY:

From Garry: Other translations of today's passage are:

- The Message Bible says, "Life collapses on loafers; lazybones go hungry," (Proverbs 19:15 [MSG]).
- The Common English Bible states: "Laziness brings on deep sleep; a slacker goes hungry," (Proverbs 19:15 [CEB]).
- The Passion Translation says, "Go ahead—be lazy and passive. But you'll go hungry if you live that way," (Proverbs 19:15 [TPT]).

Below are other proverbs that relate to today's Scripture:

- Proverbs 6:9-11 (ESV) says, "How long will you lie there, O sluggard? When will you arise from your sleep? A little sleep, a little slumber, a little folding of the hands to rest, and poverty will come upon you like a robber, and want like an armed man."
- Proverbs 12:27 (ESV) says, "Whoever is slothful will not roast his game, but the diligent man will get precious wealth."
- Proverbs 24:30-34 (ESV) says, "I passed by the field of a sluggard, by the vineyard of a man lacking sense, and behold, it was all overgrown with thorns; the ground was covered with nettles, and its stone wall was broken down. Then I saw and considered it; I looked and received instruction. A little sleep, a little slumber, a

little folding of the hands to rest, and poverty will come upon you like a robber, and want like an armed man."

A wise man will learn, but the sluggard has a way of making one excuse after another, and eventually, it just lulls him to sleep.

From Ward: The authors of Proverbs make several statements about work and laziness. I guess the authors saw much of both actions in their community. We should not confuse laziness with procrastination, poor health, or oppression. People who are surrounded by desperate situations like starvation, imprisonment, and being refugees often lose hope when work choices are not available. Those in such circumstances should not be labeled as lazy.

As our society becomes wealthier, the choices for employment increase. Being overwhelmed by all the options happens. As the culture develops defined classes, diligent work does not seem to gain an average person prestige or greater wealth. Laziness develops because focused work seems to provide little advantage. Furthermore, if protections from homelessness and starvation are easily accessible through family, friends, coworkers, and the government, then laziness is reinforced.

We should not judge those who work slower than us as lazy. We should not be angry or bitter at those who seem to earn a living with less effort than we do. God does not call us to compare and evaluate others' lives. If we believe a person is lazy, we should offer help and encouragement. Thinking derisive thoughts about our neighbor has never brought about change. Our work focus should be what 1 Timothy 6:8 (NIV) says, "But if we have food and clothing, we will be content with that." Let all remember to "…work heartily, as for the Lord and not for men," (Colossians 3:23b [ESV]), and not give worry to those we view as lazy.

From Frank: If you snooze, you lose.

From Leslie: I think you can add procrastination to this. Lord, help me not to procrastinate on the things that I need to get done. That's right up there with laziness.

From Cindi: Lord, direct my time appropriately. Show me what needs doing to glorify You. I spent many years rushing about with too much to accomplish, and I left no time for rest and reflection. Keep me balanced and productive. Amen

From Cynthia: It is a blessing to work and a blessing to volunteer for others. Children don't always get praised for their efforts at school. So, when I see a chance to encourage or recognize work in people, I'm hoping they will, in turn, pass it on. When we are teaching music and art, we are teaching that effort is valued. Work is worth doing, and people are worth recognition. It matters what people think of others. Motivation comes from the heart. The church grows when everyone is working for the Lord.

From Jim: The same is true for our spiritual growth.

From Doreen: This goes along with Proverbs 10:4, as well as several other verses in the Bible. Laziness is not suitable for life. I heard a quote that said, "Laziness breeds lethargy, and exercise (movement) breeds energy."

PRAYER:

Lord, help me not be lazy and just postpone one thing after another. May I not make excuses and be irresponsible. Amen.

CHALLENGE:

Get up. Do what you need to do!

_____
_____
_____

KEEPING YOUR LIFE

 **TODAY'S PASSAGE:**

Whoever keeps the commandment keeps his life; he who despises his ways will die.

Proverbs 19:16

COMMENTARY:

From Garry: The Catholic Public Domain Version of this proverb is: "Whoever guards a commandment guards his own soul. But whoever neglects his own way will die," (Proverbs 19:16 [CPDV]). Following through is worth it. Pay attention to the ways of God. Staying focused and being true to God will protect you. Choose life, not death. You will guard your life if you keep God's ways. It leads to fulfillment.

But disregard the ways of the Lord, and what you get will be less of life. It will be the way of death. In 1 Timothy 4:7-8 (ESV), Paul encouraged Timothy: "Have nothing to do with irreverent, silly myths. Rather train yourself for godliness; for while bodily training is of some value, godliness is of value in every way, as it holds promise for the present life and also for the life to come."

1 Timothy 6:11-12 (ESV) says, "But as for you, O man of God, flee these things. Pursue righteousness, godliness, faith, love, steadfastness, gentleness. Fight the good fight of the faith. Take hold of the eternal life to which you were called and about which you made the good confession in the presence of many witnesses."

From Ward: Keeping the commandments of God is something I have always wanted to do. I have desired this since I was a child. This differed from many children. I enjoyed going to church and singing hymns, and I did not outwardly rebel against my parents. I think many people were not like this when they lived with their parents.

No matter the age of the person reading this, I assume the reader wants to be drawn closer to God. Your past, your youth, and your young adulthood are not a concern for what you want today. This proverb has a statement and a result: if you do the commandments, you will have life. Real life. A rewarding life. A life that works. Yes, there will be pain, loss, and suffering, but God is with you during life. To do the commandments, you must know the commandments. We cannot follow God's rules if we do not know what the rules are.

How do we know the rules? We must read the Bible, hear good, sound teachings, and talk with our faithful friends. This is not just learning the Ten Commandments in Exodus 20. There are rules for our behavior throughout the Bible. Unfortunately, today, not all Christian music is biblically correct. Listening to Christian music can be helpful, but the lyrics are not always accurate.

Going to Bible studies about prayer is no longer something I want to do. No more lessons are needed about what the word *love* means in the Bible. I have heard enough sermons about the Sermon on the Mount in Matthew 5–7. What I need is to *do* the commandments. Follow the rules. Obey the guidelines.

In 1 Thessalonians 5:14b (NKJV), Paul writes, "Be patient with all." It is unnecessary for me to do a word study on the words, *patient* and *all*. I just need to *be* patient. That is my goal. When Peter writes in 1 Peter 5:6a (NKJV), "Therefore humble yourselves," I need to be humble and do this every day. We learn the commandments and rules not to earn points for a game but to grow closer to God and to produce godliness inside us. God does not keep track of how many Bible verses we remember, even if a Sunday School teacher did. One of His goals for us is to "have fervent love for one another" (1 Peter 4:8 [NKJV]). We can do that as we learn His guidelines and follow them, too. May each person reading this devotion have a deep desire to learn what God wants and ask for His grace to do those tasks.

From Leslie: We know what the greatest commandment is. Jesus said it was to "...love the Lord your God with all your heart and with all your soul and with all your strength and with all your mind," (Luke 10:27a [ESV]). So, to keep the commandments is to indeed keep our life. Jesus also said, "I am the way, and the truth, and the life. No one comes to the Father except through me," (John 14:6b [ESV]). In a nutshell, Christ is our life.

From Frank: Amen. That's the least we can do—our "reasonable service," (Romans 12:1b [NKJV]).

From Doreen: Some people don't see the value of living a godly lifestyle. Some say things like, "You're trying to be perfect," or "You act like a Pollyanna." Life is richer when you try to live a good, clean life. Everyone will make mistakes until they die. It's not about perfection but about integrity.

From Jim: We need spiritual discipline along with physical discipline in life. Perhaps we need to teach this more in our time and culture.

From Cynthia: It is difficult for me to believe that anyone could despise God's teachings and His Way. We are to flee from wrong action, and yet evil flees from us occasionally. There are so many distractions that we forget that life's all about guarding souls. We are commanded to love one another, especially if we wish to represent Christ Jesus, our Lord and Savior. Every soul is precious and worth saving.

From Cindi: Let us be vigilant and on guard! Complacency leaves us vulnerable to the enemy!

PRAYER:

Lord, thank You that You came to give us the fullness of life. You offer us life in its abundance. Help us not settle for less. Amen.

CHALLENGE:

Choose life and choose God's ways.

_____
_____
_____
_____
_____
_____
_____

LENDING A HAND

 TODAY'S PASSAGE:

> *Whoever is generous to the poor lends to the LORD, and he will repay him for his deed.*
>
> **Proverbs 19:17**

COMMENTARY:

From Garry: Note these versions and related Scriptures for today's passage:

- The Contemporary English Version says, "Caring for the poor is lending to the LORD, and you will be well repaid," (Proverbs 19:17 [CEV]).
- The Message Bible says, "Mercy to the needy is a loan to GOD and GOD pays back those loans in full," (Proverbs 19:17 [MSG]).
- Jesus taught us in Luke 6:38 (ESV) to "give, and it will be given to you. Good measure, pressed down, shaken together, running over, will be put into your lap. For with the measure, you use it will be measured back to you."
- Proverbs 14:31 (ESV) says, "Whoever oppresses a poor man insults his Maker, but he who is generous to the needy honors him."
- Proverbs 17:5 (ESV) says, " Whoever mocks the poor insults his Maker; he who is glad at calamity will not go unpunished."

God loves all people. God is especially concerned about those who are oppressed and poor. God's heart goes out to all in need. There is a story about a man who wanted to get close to the God of heaven. He thought that if he could climb up a very high ladder, he could get closer to God. He made his way all the way to the top of the ladder that was surrounded by the clouds. Once at the top, he cried out: "God, where are You?" Then he heard a voice calling up from way down below him: "I am down here, among all the people!" God is pleased when we are generous to those in need!

From Ward: I always think my possessions are mine. But they really are on loan to me from God. When I die, all I have will go to someone else. Psalm 24:1a (NIV) says, "The earth is the LORD'S and everything in it." This makes me a manager of what the Lord has given me. And one duty of that management is caring for the impoverished. This proverb reminds us that we will be repaid by the Lord for the good we do for the poor. The repayment is not always in goods or with money. Good will come to us as we remember the destitute in our community.

The church my wife and I attend has an outreach to the homeless downtown, two mornings each week. Our church does not have much to offer each time—some food, a T-shirt, and hygiene items. Yet the men and women who come to thank us are grateful for a chance to sit inside and drink coffee for a short while. Several clients have said we are genuine in our care and compassion for the homeless. Receiving respect and kindness matters more than the items they receive. Caring for the poor includes showing you recognize them as people and are not just handing items to them.

In the United States, most of us have been given and earned many possessions and money. This abundance is not just for our own happiness and contentment. God wants our wealth to be available to the needy. God wants us to be generous, not greedy. In Matthew 24, the story of the separations of the nations reminds us that God evaluates us based on our generosity. He is concerned with how much we help those who cannot get out of their miserable situation, not with how much we have in a storage unit. Let none of us forget our responsibility to assist the truly needy.

From John: I had the pleasure of being married to a woman for over 50 years who placed a high priority on helping others. She would help or tell me to help pay for a person's groceries while we were in line to check out. When she asked a person if they were all right, she was truly interested to see if they needed help. Through her, we helped many people, and whatever we gave away was returned many times over through blessings from our Lord. We are to help in every way we can; that is what Jesus taught us!

From Doreen: So true! God has blessed us so much for helping others who can't return the favor. Paying it forward is rewarding in many ways.

From Cindi: When we realize that all we have been given is from God, we use our gifts to bring hope and comfort to those in need. We do this out of love and service to the One who saved us. Otherwise, we become greedy, self-serving, and unable to hear God directing us to help.

PRAYER:

Father, make me like You. You are generous and kind. Give me a heart for people, especially those who could use a helping hand. Amen.

CHALLENGE:

Be gracious, be generous, lend a hand to the poor. You are lending to the Lord. God will bless you for it.

_____
_____
_____
_____
_____
_____
_____

GOOD GUIDANCE

TODAY'S PASSAGE:

Discipline your son, for there is hope; do not set your heart on putting him to death.

Proverbs 19:18

COMMENTARY:

From Garry: Proverbs 12:1 (ESV) says, "Whoever loves discipline loves knowledge, but he who hates reproof is stupid." The word *discipline*, for many, often has negative connotations because we associate it with pain or punishment. I like to think of discipline as *guidance*. If a parent withholds discipline, that is neither a compliment nor a kindness. It is more of a disservice to the child.

However, discipline that is too harsh does not help either. Ephesians 6:4 (ESV) says, "Fathers, do not provoke your children to anger, but bring them up in the discipline and instruction of the Lord." Preventive discipline is spending time and building a good relationship with them so that when they are corrected, they listen and learn. Corrective discipline is more helpful when it is preceded by preventive discipline.

A good home life is all about a godly example and relationships that honor God. Dr. Paul Meier, in his book *Christian Child-Rearing and Personality Development*, writes that there are five factors found in mentally healthy homes. They are:

Love - Discipline - Consistency - Example - The father leading the home

From Ward: Discipline can mean training with the objective of developing self-control. If the instructor must continually watch the students to ensure their behavior is correct, then no self-control is being developed. The purpose of good discipline is so that the trainee does what is right when no one is watching. Integrity and good conduct are the preferred results.

In our current US culture, good conduct and self-control do not seem to be favored choices. Limits, laws, and regulations are for someone else and not me. One phrase I have heard is, "I can do whatever I want as long as it does not hurt someone." This implies that we can always look into the future and determine the consequences of our deeds. When our actions hurt another person, the person says, "I'm sorry," but there is no repentance and no change in their behavior. The second person was hurt because "they got in the way," rather than my actions causing them pain, discomfort, or loss.

What a selfish world we live in! Our minds determine right and wrong, not God. Self-control takes away our fun. Limits make life boring. Jesus did not act this way. His goal was to do his Father's will and to show us how to love one another. Discipline, training, and education show us how to accomplish these goals. Ignoring others and pushing them to the side to achieve our own happiness was never God's plan. Let us encourage each other to know what God wants and to encourage others to follow those rules.

From Cynthia: Most people realize that their parents did the best they could to give them a great start in life. But from the moment we're born, the world deceives us. We are surrounded by false hopes and dreams powered by greed and screen time. All people need time with each other, and we learn that through repetition, good choices, good habits, and discipline.

The world's "systems" shouldn't be a substitute for teaching our children. I can't go back in time and be a better parent, but going forward I have the opportunity to treat every person in my life as a child of God. Writing notes of encouragement and letting our adult children know they matter is a step towards redeeming the time that we may have lost. It's never too late to change.

From Kyle: *Bibleref.com* (https://www.bibleref.com/Proverbs/19/Proverbs-19-18.html) has this to say about Proverbs 19:18:

This is one of the few biblical proverbs phrased as a command rather than a simple statement or a piece of sage advice. Parents know all too well—and some all too late—that the best time to shape a child's behavior is when they are young. This requires discipline. The meaning here is not about corporal punishment, i.e., spanking, but the overall concept of boundaries and consequences. A child left without discipline grows into an adult without respect for authority. They may struggle with self-control and decision-making. That brings the son or daughter suffering and piles shame on the parents (Proverbs 10:1). Deeply rebellious people are at much greater risk, including legal consequences (Deuteronomy 21:18–21).

Author Terri Gillespie says this about today's passage (as taken from https://authorterrigillespie.com/daily-word-balance-proverbs-1918/):

This literal translation of the Hebrew is said to be, "Do not lift up thy soul." Meaning, a caution to not chastise in anger. It's not too far of a step into, "do not abuse your child." Interesting. For every over-indulgent parent, there are those who are so angry the punishment turns to abuse.

From Barrett: This verse evokes in my mind the late 1960s/1970s and the rise of permissive parenting. Along with that comes the decline of discipline in children and a lack of respect for others' authority, particularly.

Most vividly, I remember a father whose young son was kicking him in the shins as hard as he appeared able to, again and again, in a shopping mall. The father was asking him why he was kicking him. Had he (the father) done something wrong? Was the boy angry about something else? The boy did not reply, but just kept on kicking his father as hard as he could. I walked on. I certainly believe the boy came to understand, before too many years had passed, that his father was likely the only person who would not respond in kind.

From Doreen: Undisciplined kids have a hard life because they're not taught right behavior from wrong. They may find themselves in trouble more frequently than others as kids and adults.

From Cindi: My parents had a very authoritarian style of parenting. It could sometimes be tough. Despite it all, my siblings and I turned out okay! Even when it was hard on us, we always knew we were loved. Being a teacher and a parent, what I know is true is that those kids whose parents indulge or ignore rather than discipline are the ones with the most problems. I think this proverb tells us it is a parent's responsibility to show their kids how to live in the community with others. By today's standards, you'll be considered strict!

PRAYER:

Lord, help me be a Godly parent to my children, instilling Godly values. Amen.

CHALLENGE:

Dr. Jim Jackson, former pastor of Chapelwood United Methodist Church, wrote a devotional book containing the message below:

> *My sons are raised, but if I could start all over with parenting, I would do it differently. I would finger-paint more and point the finger of blame less often. I would do less correcting and more connecting. I would take my eyes off my watch, and I would watch my kids. I would be less serious and play more. I would do more hugging and less tugging. I would be less firm and more affirming. I would put my children ahead of my career. I would be less controlling and more trusting. I would talk less and pray more. I would care less about what other people thought and care more that they knew I cared about*

them. I would enjoy being present with my child more and be less anxious about what is going to happen in the future.

ANGER

TODAY'S PASSAGE:

> *A man of great wrath will pay the penalty, for if you deliver him, you will only have to do it again.*
>
> **Proverbs 19:19**

COMMENTARY:

From Garry: The New Living Translation says, "Hot-tempered people must pay the penalty. If you rescue them once, you will have to do it again," (Proverbs 19:19 [NLT]). This proverb warns one against anger, especially when it becomes a pattern of behavior. A bad temper repeatedly gets one into trouble. Consider this: outbursts of anger almost always cause hurt feelings and irrational comments. The Bible warns against this. Look at the following verses:

- Proverbs 12:18 (ESV) says, "There is one whose rash words are like sword thrusts, but the tongue of the wise brings healing."
- Ecclesiastes 7:9 (ESV) says, "Be not quick in your spirit to become angry, for anger lodges in the heart of fools."
- Proverbs 29:22 (ESV) says, "A man of wrath stirs up strife, and one given to anger causes much transgression."
- Psalm 37:8 (ESV) says, "Refrain from anger and forsake wrath! Fret not yourself; it tends only to evil."

Because anger usually causes problems, many Scriptures encourage us to be slow to anger:

- Proverbs 29:11 (ESV) says, "A fool gives full vent to his spirit, but a wise man quietly holds it back."

- James 1:19-20 (ESV) says, "Know this, my beloved brothers: let every person be quick to hear, slow to speak, slow to anger; for the anger of man does not produce the righteousness of God."
- Ephesians 4:31 (ESV) says, "Let all bitterness and wrath and anger and clamor and slander be put away from you, along with all malice."

From Ward: Here is another proverb that mentions anger. Today, anger is a popular emotion, just like it was when this proverb was written. With the stress in our current lives, the temptation to be angry often comes. When I get angry, I generally allow this emotion to take charge of my mind and my speech. I raise my voice, say harsh words, and belittle people who are the focus of my wrath. Paul writes in Ephesians 4:26a (NKJV), "Be angry and do not sin." It must be possible to experience anger and not blast others with savage words.

As I mentioned in the previous devotion, self-control is also necessary for steering the temptation of anger away from strident speech. When tempted with anger, it is wise to pause before speaking. The goal of our words is not to punish others, but to "… encourage one another and build each other up," (1 Thessalonians 5:11a [NIV]). Rather than only defending ourselves when we are angry, we should also look at the situation as those around us do. None of us is God, and none of us is 100 percent correct in every circumstance.

Psychotherapist Moshe Ratson tells us,

> *You may become angry when you feel threatened, when you've been taken advantage of, when you feel rejected or disrespected, or when you are blocked from doing something that matters to you.*

Anger becomes a habit when we focus on fear, threats to us, and loss of boundaries. He reminds us that when we know why we are angry, we can pause and consciously transform our anger into personal growth.

As this proverb says, too many of us give in to anger over and over, never seeing a way not to respond with forceful words. Paul continues to tell us to "Be at peace among yourselves," (1 Thessalonians 5:13b [NKJV]) and to "be patient with all," (1 Thessalonians 5:14b [NKJV]). Dear reader, I ask that you make a commitment to focus on Paul's words in 1 Thessalonians when anger rises in your mind.

From Leslie: Note these verses as well:

- "Be angry and do not sin," (Ephesians 4:26 [NKJV]).
- "A soft answer [kind word] turns away wrath," (Proverbs 15:1 [NKJV, Emphasis Added]).

From Frank: Amen. Being teachable is so important.

From Doreen: Angry outbursts can cause hard feelings, frequently requiring apologies. Sometimes, people say very hurtful things that can't be taken back or soon forgotten.

PRAYER:

Lord, may I have self-control when my emotions run high. May I not sin. May I use restraint and be slow to anger. May I not let the sun go down on my anger. Amen

CHALLENGE:

In your behavior, bring healing, not hurt.

_____
_____
_____
_____
_____

ACCEPTING ADVICE

 **TODAY'S PASSAGE:**

Listen to advice and accept instruction, that you may gain wisdom in the future.

Proverbs 19:20

COMMENTARY:

From Garry: The New Living Translation says, "Get all the advice and instruction you can, so you will be wise for the rest of your life," (Proverbs 19:20 [NLT]). The Contemporary English Version states it this way: "Pay attention to advice and accept correction, so you can live sensibly," (Proverbs 19:20 [CEV]). In my journal, I wrote:

Wisdom comes by revelation, and it comes through the search for it. It is a search for God Himself. It involves a lifestyle of turning away from evil and turning towards the Light of God's salvation in Jesus Christ. It comes to the devoted who watch for it daily. A wise person is not proud, but teachable to the end, open to God's ways. He values truth enough to pay the price for it.

From Ward: According to my observations, people often seek advice from too many sources. The result is too many options. I have seen people who want no advice. The result is being alone when deciding. You may ask for guidance from some people who do not understand what you are experiencing and have no wisdom. Some people will only want to talk about their own experiences.

When you ask for help, find a kind, caring, trustworthy person who will not talk about you in front of others. We are not required to accept and do the actions others offer. Whenever we offer recommendations, we must be gentle and humble, not demanding the other person follow our instructions.

Sometimes, the stress of life is so high we cannot easily hear the words spinning around us. We should be sensitive to our hearer, realizing sometimes listening and receiving a hug is more important than being given a list of duties to do. Romans 12:15 (NKJV) reminds us to "Rejoice with those who rejoice and weep with those who weep." Wisdom often comes from family and friends, but it is not pushed; it is gently offered. The giver of counsel must be willing to have their words rejected. None of us is a master of every adversity and is the sole source of remedies. All of us have had moments of indecision, and we should respect the pain and confusion others feel in those times. Being asked for our opinion is an honor. One that should not cause us to feel superior to our friends. Let all of us forsake arrogance and being overconfident when we talk to those in need.

From Doreen: We gain wisdom from experiences and, if we listen, from others. People share their experiences to help us learn and prevent us from making the same mistakes they have made. I've also gained a lot of wisdom from watching others make mistakes, in addition to the mistakes I've made.

From Cindi: As a singer and musician, I often seek *constructive* criticism from people I trust. The best performers can take advice and will improve. I am grateful that Jesus is my life coach and is always offering me His guidance and truth. The best lives are lived by hearing the loving voice of Jesus and gaining wisdom.

PRAYER:

Lord, help me be open and receptive to your Holy Spirit as I walk on the journey towards wisdom. Help me listen, learn, and grow as I make the right turns to honor You. Amen.

CHALLENGE:

Listen to the Lord's instruction. Gain wisdom.

GOD'S PURPOSE

 **TODAY'S PASSAGE:**

Many are the plans in the mind of a man, but it is the purpose of the LORD that will stand.

Proverbs 19:21

COMMENTARY:

From Garry: Consider the following translations:

- The Contemporary English Version says, "We make a lot of plans, but the LORD will do what he has decided," (Proverbs 19:21 [CEV]).
- The Easy English Bible says, "You may have lots of ideas about what you want to do. But it is the LORD'S plans that are important," (Proverbs 19:21 [EASY]).
- God's Word says, "Many plans are in the human heart, but the advice of the LORD will endure," (Proverbs 19:21 [GW]).
- The Message Bible says, "We humans keep brainstorming options and plans, but GOD'S purpose prevails," (Proverbs 19:21 [MSG]).

There can be so much on our minds. Our minds race from one matter to another as we deal with so many issues in front of us. But God's purpose stands sure, and it will be established. We can trust God. His Word is sure. His ways are sure. You can count on it.

From Ward: There is a saying today, "Do you want to make God laugh? Then tell Him your plans!" In the book of James, the author says this another way.

Come now, you who say, "Today or tomorrow we will go into such-and-such a town and spend a year there and trade and make a profit,"—yet you do not

> *know what tomorrow will bring. What is your life? For you are a mist that appears for a little time and then vanishes. Instead, you ought to say, "If the Lord wills, we will live and do this or that."*
>
> **James 4:13-15 (ESV)**

Isaiah 46:10b (ESV) says, "My counsel shall stand, and I will accomplish all my purpose." Finally, Psalm 37:5a (ESV) says, "Commit your way to the Lord."

We all make plans, and some come to pass. Some of our plans produce the outcome we want, and some do not. Our trust is in God and not in our minds or in the intelligence of others. Not every proposal needs to be presented to God. We should pause and consider what the Lord wants for the important decisions we make. The Lord clearly states that His plans and purpose will happen. We do not need to worry or be afraid. The best plans are from the Lord, even if the plan takes time to complete. Let us remember to honor God in our planning and in our actions.

From Doreen: I have learned to pray for God's will to be done, despite the way I would prefer things to go. I know He has great plans for me and sees the bigger picture.

From Cynthia: Getting stuck, having ruminating thoughts, and losing sleep have roots in low-level thinking. We are gently reminded to love God with all our heart and to seek God first. Limitless thinking is covered in God's perfect love. When something is so horrendous and beyond our comprehension, we must still our hearts and listen to God's Word. The world has complicated solutions to manufactured problems. Usually, the world's solutions are costly and messy. God asks us to rest in Him. Time spent with God is Love.

From Frank: I love what Matthew says from the television show, *The Chosen*: "I have only one thing to do today—follow Him." Yes, Lord!

From Cindi: I always knew that I was supposed to work in ministry with young people and use my musical gifts for worship. AND YET, I let plans and other people influence me to go to dental hygiene school! God put me back on the right track after four miserable years! God is good! Trust in His direction for all your plans!

PRAYER:

Lord, life can get busy and complex. But I am glad I can trust Your eternal promises and Your holy purpose. Amen.

CHALLENGE:

Lord, You have told me not to be anxious, but to live one day at a time as I seek You and Your kingdom first. Help me do that, Lord.

_____
_____
_____
_____
_____
_____
_____

A WORTHY GOAL

TODAY'S PASSAGE:

What is desired in a man is steadfast love, and a poor man is better than a liar.
                                                                    Proverbs 19:22

COMMENTARY:

From Garry: Genuine love that is steady and true is a worthy aspiration. Love and kindness are what we need. Deep down, it is what we want. Deep down, it is what we need—steadfast love. God's steadfast love never ceases. The more we reflect on this proverb, the better it is for everybody.

Is steadfast love your goal? Is that what you aspire to? It really does not matter if you have lots of possessions. What matters is that you are honest and can be counted on. Being trustworthy means following through with your commitments and not being the person who says one thing and does another. Note these translations of today's passage:

- The Free Bible Version says, "The most desirable thing in anyone is trustworthy love; it is better to be poor than a liar," (Proverbs 19:22 [FBV]).
- The Passion Translation says, "A man is charming when he displays tender mercies to others. And a lover of God who is poor and promises nothing is better than a rich liar who never keeps his promises," (Proverbs 19:22 [TPT]).
- The New Living Translation says, "Loyalty makes a person attractive. It is better to be poor than dishonest," (Proverbs 19:22 [NLT]).
- The King James Version says, "The desire of a man is his kindness: and a poor man is better than a liar," (Proverbs 19:22 [KJV]).

From Ward: How do you define love? Please take a moment and write some thoughts on the lines at the end of this devotion. When you think of love, do you think of actions you have seen, words people have said, or experiences you have had? How does the concept of love in the media differ from your concept or what Jesus said about love? Wow, these are tough questions to answer. It is OK if you cannot think of much to write. I believe many of us have heard the following comments: "Love is an action, not a feeling," and "Love is a verb."

Proverbs 17:17a (NKJV) says, "A friend loves at all times." Jesus gave few commands, and one of these is to "...love one another," (John 13:34a [NKJV])—a worthy goal for all of us. I encourage each person reading this comment for the next week to think about how to show love to the people you know and meet. And see if this changes anything in your life or circumstances.

Now, about the second part of this proverb—does the writer mean all rich people are liars? I wonder. My mother, who was a wise woman, would say, "You do not get to be super wealthy by giving all your money away." I guess I have judgments in my mind about those who are extravagantly wealthy. Are billionaires greedy, and do they hoard money? Perhaps I do not need to think those thoughts.

Jesus, in His poverty, changed this world more than the richest people of the world have. I know the Lord does not want us to lie to gain wealth, possessions, and power. Since we cannot take our wealth to heaven, we should focus our time and effort on following God's rules. Focusing only on money draws us away from others. Focusing on being godly allows us to serve our community. May all of us be truthful in our speech and be kind and helpful to our neighbors.

From Leslie: One reason we find lying so detestable is that Satan is the father of lies. He's the master liar. So, we certainly don't want to be like him. We want to be like Jesus, who is the Truth. I'm reminded of how my daddy couldn't stand a liar. He found it most detestable. We kids could get away with just about anything, but not lying!

From Doreen: Being loved makes life more bearable, especially when you have someone with whom you love to share it. Being known as a liar would probably make for a lonely life.

From Cynthia: Have you ever noticed that people who have great marriages often follow this Scripture and a couple more? It seems natural to them. An onlooker might think that it isn't fair that some are blessed with an unusually gifted marriage. These rare marriages are loyal and truthful. They cherish each other and respect each other. It sometimes looks like God blessed a few marriages, and most other people just attract the wrong people. But God is preparing us for the greatest of all relationships by helping us learn to get along with each other.

From Cindi: What a beautiful way to live! Be yourself while living with integrity and love for others!

PRAYER:

Lord, I want to be like You. May I reflect Your loyal love in all my relationships. Amen.

CHALLENGE:

The greatest adventure is following Jesus and living in the light of His love every day.

_____
_____
_____
_____
_____
_____
_____

THE FEAR OF THE LORD

 **TODAY'S PASSAGE:**

> *The fear of the LORD leads to life, and whoever has it rests satisfied; he will not be visited by harm.*
>
> **Proverbs 19:23**

COMMENTARY:

From Garry: The phrase *fear of the LORD* occurs often in the Book of Proverbs. What does it mean? It is associated with the beginning of wisdom. It is the starting place of finding the great treasure of wisdom. In two proverbs, *the fear of the LORD* is synonymous with the *knowledge of God*. Proverbs 2 says,

> *My son, if you receive my words and treasure up my commandments with you, making your ear attentive to wisdom and inclining your heart to understanding; yes, if you call out for insight and raise your voice for understanding, if you seek it like silver and search for it as for hidden treasures, then you will understand the fear of the LORD and find the knowledge of God. For the LORD gives wisdom; from his mouth come knowledge and understanding; he stores up sound wisdom for the upright; he is a shield to those who walk in integrity.*
>
> **Proverbs 2:1-7 (ESV)**

Proverbs 9:10 (ESV) says, "The fear of the LORD is the beginning of wisdom, and the knowledge of the Holy One is insight." Fearing God is knowing God. It involves a relationship of intimacy and a sense of awe in His holy presence. It is life with God. Proverbs 3 says:

> *Trust in the LORD with all your heart, and do not lean on your own understanding. In all your ways acknowledge him, and he will make straight your paths. Be not wise in your own eyes; fear the LORD and turn away from evil. It will be healing to your flesh and refreshment to your bones.*
>
> **Proverbs 3:5-8 (ESV)**

As we practice the presence of God, we discover life in its fullness. This is what a relationship with Christ is all about: knowing God and having *life*. That brings true satisfaction and fulfillment.

From Ward: What do you fear? Maybe I have asked this question before. Please take a few seconds and write on the lines at the end of this devotion any situations or people you fear or have anxiety about. I admit fear of the Lord is not on my list. I do not fear dying, but the process of dying—pain, not being able to communicate, and losing my bodily functions. When my dad was living, I had an almost constant fear of him because of his anger. I fear being embarrassed in public, too. I am sure you have many others.

The author reminds us, though, that fear, respect, admiration, and honor of the Lord are most important. Since He is the owner and creator of all of this, He deserves His respect. I need to remember this each day. I have my prayer time each day, and I remember to pray during the day. Even so, my focus during my waking hours is on the mundane chores of living. I wonder if keeping a fear of the Lord in mind during the day would change my attitude. My challenge to you is, "What would your day be like if you kept a fear of the Lord in your mind all day?"

Now, about the second part of this proverb—"he will not be visited by harm." This is a *principle*, not a *promise*. God does not prevent all harm. Many of us are quickly protected from pain and loss, but many Christians are not. One statement I heard in the past is "More 20th-century Christians died for their faith than in the previous 19 centuries combined." I believe this.

While God has a desire for his people not to suffer violence and injury, He does not promise this to every Christian alive. Jesus died on the cross and was resurrected to validate our trust in God. Our trust is in His eternal love for us, not in any prosperity, success, or peaceful circumstance we have now.

- Our trust is knowing we will be in His eternal kingdom after death, not enjoying a stress-free life today.
- Our trust is in His eternal plan for us, not the temporary choices of living.

May the fear of the Lord provide wisdom and peace for us each day.

From Frank H.: Fear of the Lord is the beginning of wisdom, knowledge, and relationship with Him. Following God's plan is always better than following our own.

From Frank C.: Such wisdom here! We need to realize there is a God, and it's not us!

From Doreen: Life is not perfect for believers in Christ. However, we have a much better life knowing that God is always near to help us through whatever challenges come our way. I can honestly say that since I have made my relationship with God, spending time with Him, and studying my Bible a priority, my life is so much better. I very seldom worry, and my faith is a lot stronger. The Bible is such an amazing book of instructions for living life.

From Cynthia: Comparing ourselves is one side effect of fear gone wrong. Each night, I'm sobered by the realization that I haven't sought or done God's will. We make better choices when the wisdom of God is sought after every day. Most negativity is spawned from fear, but the fear of the Lord is positive in the light of love and wisdom.

From Barrett: To me, the two phrases that follow are diametrically opposed to loving God as a Christian.

- "The fear of the LORD leads to life and whoever has it rests satisfied," (Proverbs 19:23a [ESV]).

- "The fear of the LORD is the beginning of knowledge," (Proverbs 1:7 [ESV]).

Reading the Bible has never instilled in me a sense that equates the two: love God and fear God.

I can understand the inveterate sinner who curses God, who hates the idea of God, fearing Him. But to fear Him in that regard must also mean that he believes in God, or there would be no one, nothing there to fear. The unrepentant sinner who does not believe has no reason to fear Him.

Far better, and it seems to me more accurate, should be, "The *LOVE* of the LORD leads to life, and whoever has it rests satisfied." And "*LOVE* the Lord. That is the beginning of knowledge." We are His children, and children occasionally, and probably deservedly, fear their father coming home. Do we fear His coming? Should we fear His coming? Better in my mind to *love* the Lord and not fear Him, for *HE* loves us—all of us.

Fearing our name is not found in The Book of Life is terrifying—if we believe in God, in satan, in hell. Perhaps Bible verses about fearing God address sinful believers.

PRAYER:

Father, I want to know You and love You. I want to seek You with all my heart. Help me honor You. Amen.

CHALLENGE:

The motto in Proverbs is to fear the Lord. That is the beginning of knowledge. There is nothing better than knowing the Lord.

_____
_____
_____

THE POOR SLUGGARD

 **TODAY'S PASSAGE:**

The sluggard buries his hand in the dish and will not even bring it back to his mouth.

Proverbs 19:24

COMMENTARY:

From Garry: The Message Bible says, "Some people dig a fork into the pie but are too lazy to raise it to their mouth," (Proverbs 19:24 [MSG]). A similar proverb is Proverbs 26:15 (ESV): "The sluggard buries his hand in the dish; it wears him out to bring it back to his mouth."

When we ask a sluggard a question that pertains to a matter, he does not get started on it. But if he does, he does not finish the matter. The sluggard will not even finish eating his meal, so his food gets cold. What he sees in front of him is nothing but excuses, as he rationalizes his own laziness. As a result, he is restless and has unfulfilled desires. He is helpless amid all his small amount of activity. He is useless to those who ask him to get a job done. He is a sad picture of laziness.

From Ward: The sluggard is not the same as a poor person. The poor may not have many possessions or resources, but they still work and seek to provide for their family. The sluggard does not make any effort to maintain himself. The picture is of someone who does not care about their situation. We should see the difference between those who seek help and those who just sit and have no initiative.

God gave us the Sabbath as a day of rest for each week. It is wise to observe the Sabbath and take time each day to talk to the Lord. However, staying idle 24 hours a day is not emotionally healthy.

This is true spiritually, too. God's favor is on those who are part of His plan. God's best gifts rarely come to those who ignore Him. We were created by God and placed in a garden. Our responsibility in the garden was "to work it and take care of it," (Genesis 2:15b [NIV]). God did not intend for those of us who can work to sit and be totally unproductive each day. Even those who are physically disabled can always pray. Let us not be like the sluggard who only thinks of himself and what others can give him. Let us see each opportunity for each day to praise and give glory to the Lord in whatever way we can.

From Doreen: A lazy person doesn't have the ambition to achieve anything. I don't understand this type of person. You don't have to have gigantic dreams. You can be successful at running your own household well if that's the season of life that you're in. Based on my education, I do know that some people do not have the energy to do anything because they have a poor diet.

From Cindi: That attitude makes me anxious!

From Cynthia: Della and Joe Sanders were two of the most generous and productive people I have known. Age or health were never excuses not to work or help others. They always volunteered to help, even when you didn't know you needed help. They didn't have children but had compassion and time for so many people. They made it difficult to be a sluggard or to exhibit any kind of procrastination in their presence. They taught positive habits and behavior by example because of their faith in Jesus. We need to encourage others so they understand they can conquer their own problems with faith and resilience.

From Frank: Some people are so lazy that they don't complete any tasks, not even eating. They are useless to everyone, including themselves.

PRAYER:

Lord, deliver me from a lazy life. Amen.

CHALLENGE:

Don't just sit there; get up and do something!

A SCOFFER

 **TODAY'S PASSAGE:**

Strike a scoffer, and the simple will learn prudence; reprove a man of understanding, and he will gain knowledge. He who does violence to his father and chases away his mother is a son who brings shame and reproach. Cease to hear instruction, my son, and you will stray from the words of knowledge. A worthless witness mocks at justice, and the mouth of the wicked devours iniquity. Condemnation is ready for scoffers, and beating for the backs of fools.
Proverbs 19:25-29

COMMENTARY:

From Garry: A scoffer in the Bible describes a person who arrogantly mocks and rejects God and His teachings. They usually employ sarcasm and cruelty, belittling those who follow God. Their mind stubbornly refuses to be open to the truth. A wise person is open to reason and learns from those who are confronted with the truth. A scoffer in the family refuses to listen to the parents' advice. As a result, they stray from wisdom. In their arrogance, they lose sight of what is fair. They think they know better than everyone else. They cause problems because they distort the truth.

From Ward: For the last devotion of this book, I want to write about instruction. The author of these proverbs is intent on wanting the reader to know that we should be peaceful in receiving information. I have seen many adults who are more interested in speaking their own opinions and not listening to others. We are not required to agree with all the words we hear. But God does want us to be polite, gentle, and patient in our behavior.

When I was much younger, I thought that after reaching a certain age, there would be nothing more to learn. As years passed by, I quickly realized that learning occurs every year. This includes reinforcement of what is true, adding new information, and rearranging our understanding. God's wisdom and truth are eternal. Yet, I still get new insights even after retirement. If only I had it all together—but if so, I would not know where to put it!

For myself, I want to discern between what is true and what is false and not belittle those I disagree with. I trust God will show me wisdom, truth, and correct knowledge if I take time to listen and focus on His words in the Bible. May all of us reject scoffing and "as far as it depends on you, live at peace with everyone," (Romans 12:18b [NIV]).

From Cindi: I'm tempted to say, "I told you so," when it turns out I was right about something, and my husband or children were wrong—kind of "scoffer-like!" Then I remember I can be wrong sometimes, and wouldn't want them to rub it in. It reminds me of the old song, "Oh Lord, it's hard to be humble when you're perfect in every way" ("It's Hard to Be Humble" by Mac Davis). Seriously, Dear Lord, keep my heart pure and humble.

From Cynthia: This is a cautionary tale for parents, children, judges, lawyers, and anyone who thinks they know everything they need to know about anything. Pride gets in the way of good choices.

From Frank: Excellent challenge—it takes very little to scoff or to mock; it takes an open heart to love.

PRAYER:

Lord, do not let me become proud or arrogant, thinking I have the answer. Give me humility and an open mind. Amen.

CHALLENGE:

Think about what Psalm 1:1-2 says:

> *Blessed is the man who walks not in the counsel of the wicked, nor stands in the way of sinners, nor sits in the seat of scoffers; but his delight is in the law of the LORD, and on his law he meditates day and night.*
>
> **Psalm 1:1-2 (ESV)**

_____

_____

_____

_____

_____

_____

_____

_____

ABOUT THE AUTHORS

Garry Masterson is a retired United Methodist minister after 38 years in pulpit ministry. As a graduate of the University of Texas with a Bachelor of Fine Arts, he continued his studies at Southern Methodist University. There, he earned a Master of Divinity from the Perkins School of Theology. As an elder in the Global Methodist Church, Garry is a part-time associate pastor at Christ Church in College Station, TX.

Outside of his ministerial duties, Garry enjoys gardening and painting. He created the art that became the background for this book's cover. He and his wife, Cindy, have two sons and four grandchildren. The Mastersons live in Bryan, TX.

Ward Schmidt is a native Texan, graduating with a BA in History Teacher Education from the University of Houston and an MA in History from the University of Texas, Austin. His teaching career began in Houston's east end, at a local school district within a Christian community where he met his wife, Iris Ann. Ward's second career was in administration at a scientific instruments company until his retirement in 2017.

The Schmidts have been married for over 43 years and have three daughters and one grandson. Ward is an active volunteer for First Methodist Church in downtown Houston, leading mission trips, teaching Sunday School, and serving the homeless community.

MEET THE CONTRIBUTORS

Cindy Masterson is Garry's sweet wife. They have been married for 47 years and have two sons, Josh and Sam, as well as four grandchildren. Cindy was the inspiration for a book studying the wisdom of Proverbs. She is also an author, having written four Bible Studies on Salvation, Healing, and Equipping, as well as a book on prayer titled *Our Father, Praying Like Jesus*.

Doreen VanDyke is a lifelong Methodist who loves getting out to enjoy God's creation. She loves rock climbing, saltwater fishing, trail running, camping, and hiking. She is also a nutrition and wellness advisor who understands the health benefits of exercise and being in nature. She's been married to her best friend for over 32 years; they have two adult sons.

Cindi Cicio was born and raised in Beaumont, TX. She graduated from Lamar University and attended SMU Perkins School of Theology. A vocalist, pianist, and worship leader, she has also directed youth and children's ministries. Cindy also taught music in both public and private schools. She and her husband, Patrick, live in Spring, TX, and enjoy spending time with family and traveling.

Rev. Frank Coats, shown here with his wife Brenda, is a retired Methodist pastor. He still serves the Lord and His church.

Cynthia Lara miraculously overcame a severe allergy to books in the fourth grade. She is affectionately known as "Oma" to two boys who love her dearly.

Rev. John E. Burchell has retired as a full-time UMC Minister and now serves two churches in Leon County, TX, as an elder in the Global Methodist Church. John and his wife, Sally, were married for over 50 years before she passed in October 2024. During her last few months, he taught the Bible to the residents of Focused Care in Huntsville, TX., where he still conducts weekly church services. John has three children, eight grandchildren, and eight great-grandchildren. He enjoys playing golf and enjoying the beauty of nature, as he lives in Huntsville.

Leslie Herndon came to know the Lord at nine years of age. She grew up in the Baptist Church and has been a Baptist all her life. For over 30 years, Leslie and her husband have enjoyed leading their adult Bible study. Prior to her 25-year career as a financial advisor, she taught high school for twelve years.

Rev. Kelley G. Sexton is an ordained elder in the Global Methodist Church and Senior Pastor at 1st Methodist Church in Normangee, TX. He and his wife, Tammy, have been married for 42 years and have three grown children. The Sextons love God's great creation and spending time outdoors through traveling, hiking, boating, hunting, and fishing.

Rev. Bruce Wood is a retired United Methodist pastor, having served pastorates in the Texas Conference. He has been married to his wife, Connie, for over 55 years, and they live in College Station, TX. Bruce and Connie are active in sharing Christ and living for the glory of God.

Rev. Kyle McNelly is a Methodist minister and a good friend of the authors. He is married to Karen, and they live in College Station, TX. Each week, Kyle joins a Global Methodist Clergy Band Group for prayer and mutual encouragement.

Frank Hons is a retired professor from Texas A&M University. Frank and his wife, Tami, are active in Christ Church, College Station. Frank leads a men's group and Bible study there. He is a dedicated Christian who loves the Lord.

Myra Allison is a good friend and sister-in-Christ to the author. She inspires people with her dedication and commitment to the Lord. As a member of Grace Bible Church, she often hosts Bible studies there. Myra is married to Barrett Allison (another contributor to this book).

Barrett Allison is a retired engineer and a dedicated layperson who serves the Lord well. His deep thinking and well-read gifts were a valuable contribution to these Proverbs conversations. He is married to Myra Allison, who also contributed to this book.

Wright G. Doyle and his wife, Dori, have been married for 57 years. They served as missionaries in Taiwan, where Wright taught Greek and New Testament classes at the China Evangelical Seminary. Wright has authored several books, including *Christ the King* and *Worship and Wisdom*. He was also the editor of *Builders of the Chinese Church*. The Doyles have also participated in a Re-Engage Group at Christ Church.

Rev. Jim Jackson is the pastor of First Methodist Church in Madisonville, TX. He is a humble servant of Christ within the Global Methodist Church. He is also a part of the clergy band that meets bi-weekly to encourage other pastors.

Cliff Neal is a school teacher in Houston and an active member of Sagemont Church. He holds a degree in Theology from Southwestern Baptist Theological Seminary.

CONTACT INFORMATION

For interview or speaking engagement requests, please contact the authors using the information below.

    Rev. Garry Masterson   garrymasterson@christchurchcs.org
    Ward Schmidt   wgschmidt@sbcglobal.net